W9-ACP-007

QA 76.9 .C66 B68 2000
Bowers
Le⁺

NEW ENGLAND INSTITUTE
OF TECHNOLOGY
LEARNING RESOURCES CENTER

Let Them Eat Data

OTHER BOOKS BY C. A. BOWERS

*The Progressive Educator and the Depression: The Radical Years* (1969)

*Cultural Literacy for Freedom* (1974)

*The Promise of Theory: Education and the Politics of Cultural Change* (1984)

*Elements of a Post-Liberal Theory of Education* (1987)

*The Cultural Dimensions of Educational Computing: Understanding the Non-Neutrality of Technology* (1988)

*Responsive Teaching: An Ecological Approach to Classroom Patterns of Language, Culture, and Thought* (1990, with D. Flinders)

*Critical Essays on Education, Modernity, and the Recovery of the Ecological Imperative* (1993)

*Education, Cultural Myths, and the Ecological Crisis: Toward Deep Changes* (1993)

*Educating for an Ecologically Sustainable Culture: Rethinking Moral Education, Creativity, Intelligence, and Other Modern Orthodoxies* (1995)

*The Culture of Denial: Why the Environmental Movement Needs a Strategy for Reforming Universities and Public Schools* (1997)

*Educating for Eco-Justice and Community* (forthcoming)

# Let Them Eat Data

How Computers

Affect Education,

Cultural Diversity,

and the Prospects of

Ecological Sustainability

C. A. BOWERS

NEW ENGLAND INSTITUTE
OF TECHNOLOGY
LEARNING RESOURCES CENTER

The University of Georgia Press    Athens and London

# 43694267

101

© 2000 by the University of Georgia Press

Athens, Georgia 30602

All rights reserved

Set in 10.3 on 15 Minion by G&S Typesetters

Printed and bound by Maple-Vail

The paper in this book meets the guidelines for
permanence and durability of the Committee on
Production Guidelines for Book Longevity of the
Council on Library Resources.

Printed in the United States of America

04   03   02   01   00   C   5   4   3   2   1

04   03   02   01   00   P   5   4   3   2   1

Library of Congress Cataloging-in-Publication Data

Bowers, C. A.

    Let them eat data : how computers affect education, cultural

diversity, and the prospects of ecological sustainability / C. A. Bowers.

       p. cm.

    Includes bibliographical references and index.

     ISBN 0-8203-2229-6 (alk. paper)—ISBN 0-8203-2230-X

(pbk.: alk. paper)

     1. Computers and civilization.   2. Education—Data processing.

I. Title.

QA76.9.C66 B68 2000

303.48′34—dc21                                        00-026718

British Library Cataloging-in-Publication Data available

# Contents

# Acknowledgments

*Let Them Eat Data* is the outgrowth of many influences and personal experiences, which included encountering the perceptions of how computers are being viewed in cultures in South Africa, Asia, Mexico, and the indigenous cultures of the American Southwest. The question of whether the proponents of educational computing understood the broader educational and cultural implications first became a concern in the late 1980s as I watched the proliferation of computer education courses that failed to engage issues surrounding the most dominant characteristic of a computer: It is a cultural mediating and thus transforming technology. Concerns about the vision of a global culture based on computer-related technologies that continue to be promoted in books and through the media became more central as I began to learn how Third World writers were questioning the Western approach to technological and economic development. My more long-standing focus of attention, which has been on writing about how the educational process reproduces the cultural patterns that are exacerbating the ecological crisis, became a major source of motivation for writing a book that examines the linkages between computer-mediated learning and the spread of environmentally destructive cultural patterns and practices.

But books never spring from the head of an autonomous thinker. Conversations with scholars and activists who share similar concerns, years of reading over a wide area of related topics, and conducting graduate seminars where ideas were questioned and refined, all had an important influence. The scholar-activists whose conversations and books have been especially useful include Fritjof Capra, Alan Drengson, Harold Glasser, Andrew Kimbrell, Jerry Mander, Helena Norberg-Hodge, George Sessions, Vandana Shiva, Charlene Spretnak, and Langdon Winner. The many opportunities to learn from them can be traced to the Foundation for Deep Ecology, which brought together on a fairly regular basis scholar-activists who are addressing global issues from a deep ecology perspective. Students in the doctoral specialization of Community and Environmental Renewal at Portland State University who have helped in the clarification of ideas include Bill Bigelow, Eric Brattain, Jeff Edmundson, Stephen Gilchrist, Shelley Simon, Andrea Smith, and Robyn Voetterl.

The support given by my wife, Mary Katharine Bowers, has taken many forms, including suggestions for making parts of the analysis more lucid and sharing insights and perspectives on issues that I had overlooked. Also appreciated is the awareness on the part of Barbara Ras, executive editor of the University of Georgia Press, that the book addresses the growing concerns of many parents and citizens that have not been adequately examined in a public forum. Her encouragement and suggestions for improving the manuscript have been especially useful. A special debt is owed to copyeditor Marcella Friel for suggesting changes that significantly improved the readability of the book.

# Part 1
# Cultural and
# Ecological Consequences

Nearly everyone who owns a computer has found it to be a useful technology. The uses vary from sending e-mail to relatives and professional colleagues to modeling systems and delivering university courses to storing and retrieving data connected with business operations. More generally, the "experts" who promote globalization view the computer in a more messianic light, as the technology that will create new markets and thus reduce poverty and so-called backwardness in the seemingly undeveloped parts of the world. The Information Highway, according to their vision of the future, will not only increase efficiency in creating more goods and services within a shrinking resource base but will also contribute to the disappearance of traditional cultures—just as the interstate highway system led to the demise of local communities that could not join the new economic order.

There are several major flaws in this line of thinking. The most significant is that computers embody the double binds experienced by the cultures that created them and that are now giving them a central role in the messianic project of modernization. Because a double bind encompasses both benefits and drawbacks, and because we usually focus only on the benefits, the drawbacks often go unnoticed. For example, the Industrial Revolution raised the material standard of living and brought many conveniences into the lives of ordinary people; but its success depended on the destruction of self-sufficient and symbolically rich cultures, turned much of the environment into a wasteland, and put the world on its current environmentally destructive pathway.

Another example of a double bind lies in how science, on the one hand, advances our understanding of the natural world and increases our technological prowess while, on the other hand, it de-legitimates the mythopoetic narratives of morally coherent cultures and thus contributes to the moral relativism that accelerates consumer society. Similarly, computers have many useful applications and have even helped renew the myth of progress tarnished by two world wars and by governments' inability to bridge the widening gulf between the rich and the poor. However, the mesmerizing rate of technological innovation and the challenges of their different applications have prevented us from recognizing the computer's peculiar double bind. The following analysis of the double binds that computers create—with ourselves, our communities, and the natural environment—will help us recognize the danger of thinking of computers only within the framework of their personal use and within the myth of progress that surrounds them.

# 1 Globalizing Cyberspace: Vision and Reality

The Palacio de Justicia in the Mexican city of Morelia offers its visitors conflicting cultural messages: while the Spanish colonial architecture communicates a sense of permanence to the graceful stone arches and inner courtyard, and a huge mural depicting the heroes of Mexican independence dominates the central staircase, across the Calle de Allende toward the entrance to the palace one sees banners protesting the 1995 government decisions leading to the loss of ancestral lands, and sleeping cots under the archway where a small group of Indians are in their thirtieth day of a hunger strike. The well-dressed bureaucrats and citizens make their way into the inner courtyard without acknowledging the demonstration, while the lone police officer walking through the craft vendors' corridor gives no hint of recognition.

Similar examples of contrast can be found in nearly every region of the world: Central and South America, Africa, India, China, Southeast Asia, and North America. With the world's population increasing to over six billion since 1900 and projected to reach eight billion before stabilizing in 2030, the major challenge facing humanity will be to provide for our basic needs of food, shelter, and meaningful employment. The rapid decline in available fresh water, topsoil, forest cover, and plant and animal diversity further exacerbates our challenge. The millions of tons of toxic chemicals released into the environment, which are changing the basic chemistry of life itself, represent the less visible yet more potentially lethal and irreversible part of our dilemma of survival.

Yet we never see the gravity of these realities presented in the mainstream media, nor in the popular magazines and books intended to shape our understanding of the new consumer-oriented and environmentally destructive civilization that will result from the computer revolution. Instead, we encounter in mass media a view of technological progress as irreversible and universally benevolent. We read in magazines and see on television that the latest software, the new computer-based systems of communication and marketing, and the myriad forms of interactive entertainment (a recent one being a program that allows young girls to dress Barbie in 150 different outfits) are contributing to the general improvement of our human situation. The level of technological euphoria and the authoritative tone with which each computer-based innovation is explained to us make criticism seem unwarranted and even subversive. (Witness the growing practice of derisively labeling computer critics as neo-Luddites.) Our inability to discuss seriously the deeper implications of the experimental cultural trajectory that computers have put us on (a trajectory that began with the Industrial Revolution) reflects our educational institutions' failure to provide the conceptual frameworks necessary for understanding technology as more than a tool that enables us to achieve our goals more efficiently and as the latest expression of human evolution.

We must ask important questions about whether computers will contribute to an ecologically sustainable and culturally diverse future. Such questions, however, are largely obscured by how proponents represent the benefits of this increasingly ubiquitous technology. Note the unqualified optimism in the following claims about the changes that computers will bring:

> By combining all information—numbers, texts, sound, and images—in digital form, and making it available everywhere, and making it infinitely manipulable, the information highway will utterly change our lives (Ellison, 1994, p. 4).

Computing is not about computers anymore. It is about living. . . .
As we interconnect ourselves, many values of the nation state will
give way to those of both larger and smaller electronic communities.
We will socialize in digital neighborhoods in which physical space
will be irrelevant and time will play a different role (Negroponte,
1995, pp. 6–7).

VR [virtual reality] is an important threshold in the evolution of
human-computer symbiosis. . . . In coming years, we will be able
to put on a headset, or walk into a media room, and surround ourselves in a responsive simulation of startling verisimilitude. Our
most basic definitions of reality will be redefined in that act of perception (Rheingold, 1991, pp. 387–388).

University presidents and classroom teachers make the same
statements of relentless optimism, inevitability, and universality. The
business community shares the euphoria about the latest stage in
this supposedly evolutionary, competitive, life-forming process. Indeed, the shared optimism has led universities into collaboration
with corporations through the establishment of virtual university
degree programs and web sites for courses on many campuses across
North America. Reflecting the re-emergence of Social Darwinist
thinking among computer proponents, they show little interest in
what happens to individuals, families, and communities left in the
computer revolution's wake.

## Computerization, Environmental Integrity,
## and Cultural Continuity

Contrary to popular predictions, the next century will not be
characterized by individuals who fluidly navigate from one simulated reality to another. At least this will not be true of most of the
world's population. Instead, as many aware and responsible observers clearly see today, our future will be shaped by the environmental

trends that are already bringing into question cultural assumptions and practices.

The consequences of world population growth are now part of nearly everyone's daily experience. However, the rate and regional nature of population growth may not be as widely understood. The rapid acceleration in population, from approximately one billion in 1900 to six billion today, is continuing—with over ninety million people being added each year. Over half the world's population is concentrated in India, China, and Southeast Asia, where fresh water, agricultural lands, and local fisheries are already severely stressed. These regions are also developing modern economies and consumer expectations that will result in a rapid increase in pollution, including changes in the carbon cycle that directly influence global warming. Worldwide, demands on nonrenewable energy are expected to triple by 2025. Industrialized countries now produce millions of tons of hazardous waste and export much of it to developing countries. Synthetic chemicals that are the basis of modern technologies and consumer goods contribute to both a rapid increase in the rates of animal and plant extinction and an increased number of cancers and other health problems. The life expectancy of Russian men is declining at an alarming rate, and in North America and Western Europe scientists find a near 50 percent reduction in the sperm count among men.

Other manifestations of our declining ecological well-being clearly provide evidence that the environment—not the optimistic visions of cyberspace theorists and proponents—will be the dominant challenge of the next century.

Two other related trends ignored by computer proponents will have an adverse impact on life in the next century. The temporary expansion of jobs connected with creating the new computer infrastructure and the emphasis on the global possibilities of e-commerce have diverted attention from losses occurring in the work place and in non-consumer-based relationships. As Jeremy Rifkin emphasizes in *The End of Work* (1995), a major impact of computers on the work force is the massive elimination of the need for workers. In North America and Western Europe, the work force decline in agriculture and manufacturing has been occurring for decades. Computers accelerate the process by governing the planting and harvesting of crops, running the machines of industry, coordinating complex communication systems, and, with recent developments in biotechnology, turning the genetic engineering of new life forms into a major growth industry. Computers are making office workers redundant in both the public and private sectors and are enabling manufacturers to shift production facilities to areas of the world where labor costs are low.

The apparent gains in efficiency, like other seemingly benevolent technological changes, have a shadow side that those who promote the benefits of computer technology largely ignore. Not only do such arrangements undermine the economic viability of communities that lose industries to cheaper overseas labor markets, they introduce Western economic and technological development into Third World countries. As a result, centuries-old, sustainable traditions of craft knowledge are eroded, and self-sufficient societies become dependent on technologies that will, with further automation, introduce the same cycle experienced in the West—increased productivity with fewer and fewer workers. In effect, computers contribute to the cruel paradox of fostering greater efficiencies in the design and production of goods and services while reducing opportunities of employment.

But in most of the Third World, the loss of local traditions of production and exchange that accompanies the Western industrial style of production and consumption have far more dire consequences. These trends have immense implications for the economic and social stability of countries with growing populations. They also have important psychological implications for people who find a sense of community and self-development in more traditional approaches to work but whose work experience in the computer era too often involves adapting to the routines of systems that have few connections with traditional cultural patterns of interaction and responsibility.

The other trend suggesting that the next century will not be a cyberspace utopia is the ways in which computers accelerate the globalization of commodified relationships and knowledge. The Industrial Revolution marked a turning point in human development, with its emphasis on enabling producers to manipulate the public's sense of need and thus transform food, clothes, art, healing, education, entertainment, nature, and now even the genetic basis of life itself into commodities subject to the forces of the marketplace. The inescapable reality is that computerization commodifies whatever activities fall under its domain. Our current computer networks expand this economic and cultural orientation in ways that were previously inconceivable. Owning a computer and having access to the electronic infrastructure requires significant expenditures, which increase every time a new generation of software or hardware forces an upgrade. The equipment that enables users to enter cyberspace transforms what were previously face-to-face relationships into commodified and thus market-mediated relationships.

Computer proponents take for granted the Western myths that represent change as linear, progressive, and evolutionary and view themselves as spokespersons for an emergent universal culture, but their writings fail to acknowledge that many cultures do not want to follow the West's approach to economic and technological development. An increasing number of Third World writers are rediscovering the strengths of their own cultural traditions and challenging the prevailing vision of a new world order. In summarizing the cultural compromises that legitimize computers, Gerald Berthoud (1992) writes that "development is held to be possible only for those who are ready to rid themselves entirely of their traditions, and to devote themselves to making economic profit, at the expense of a whole gamut of social and moral obligations" (p. 70). Berthoud's statement contains two important points: one, that many cultures are centered on renewing and carrying forward their traditions and two, that these traditions are largely understood within many cultures as an ecology of moral obligations essential to a sustainable community. In his book *The Moral Economy of the Peasant: Rebellion and Subsistence in Southeast Asia* (1976), James C. Scott explains how tradition and moral obligations come together in the life of the community. He notes that "the moral principle of reciprocity permeates peasant life, and perhaps social life in general. It is based on the simple idea that one should help those who help him or (its minimalist formulation) at least not injure him" (p. 176).

While computer advocates see humanity merging into the new life form of cyborgs, cultures variously described as vernacular, indigenous, and traditional are struggling to conserve their traditions, even in the midst of urban life. For example, the Zapoteca Indians living in Mexico City continue to speak their pre-Columbian language, wear traditional dress, celebrate the traditional village fiestas, and participate indirectly as the *mayordomos* of the annual patron saint fiesta of their village. Hundreds of other indigenous cultures, ranging from the Maoris of New Zealand to the Saami in Northern Europe, do not share in a postmodern view of the individual and a technologically mediated form of community life. Nor do the cultures still influenced by Hinduism, Islam, Confucianism, and Buddhism share the Western cultural assumptions that enable computers to proliferate. Indeed, the anti-tradition thinking of computer proponents does not accurately represent how in their own lives they re-enact traditions that do not fit the patterns of cultural relativism computers reinforce. These traditions, which range from the subject-verb-object pattern of the English language to the patterns of metacommunication that frame interpersonal communication, are mostly experienced at a tacit level of awareness—that is, at a level of symbolic reality deeper than what the electronics can now digitize.

Cultural differences in ways of knowing, living, and tacitly re-enacting and renewing traditions are thus not accounted for in the legitimizing ideology and design characteristics of computers. Nevertheless, they are important because, as I describe in greater detail in later chapters, cultural traditions that have not been com-modified by technology (with all its consequences) may serve us in the technology-driven society as more environmentally sustainable examples of community life.

## *Overview of the Contents*

The chapters in this book are based on the recognition that com-puters have now become an irreversible part of cultural life in the West. This is not to say that how we represent them as technologies of empowerment is not open to debate or serious change. Indeed, one of the arguments that runs throughout the book is that because we are still in the euphoric stage of our encounter with comput-ers, we have yet to conduct a serious debate about the connections between our computer-reinforced cultural patterns and our current ecological crisis. In order to help lay the basis for this urgently needed debate, the book's chapters are organized around two related concerns.

First is the need to identify the ways in which both the design el-ements and the legitimizing ideology behind computers reinforce ecologically problematic cultural assumptions and lifestyles. Chap-ters 2 through 4 establish a conceptual framework for understand-ing how the globalization of computer-based culture is becoming an even more destructive form of colonialism than was experienced in the nineteenth century. Chapters 5 through 7 address the second concern: the educational changes we need to make in order to democratize technological innovation and use, rather than leaving these decisions to apparent experts who are primarily concerned with economic issues. Indeed, the failure of cyberspace proponents to understand how computers have effected a cultural transformation that causes us to overshoot the sustaining capacity of our natural systems and undermine culturally unique modes of knowledge points to educational shortcomings we urgently need to address.

Chapter 2 examines the cultural differences between cyberspace and everyday life. Terms such as *virtual reality* and *cyberspace* are becoming more widely used in the popular media, and even in the discourse of educational reform, in ways that suggest radically different forms of consciousness, concepts of subjectivity, and patterns of moral reciprocity. Participation in experiences not limited by historical constraints of time and space may make questioning such experiences seem unnecessary. Within the educational institutions that promote high-status forms of knowledge and certify the scientists, journalists, and other experts who promote the consumer-oriented technological culture, the pervasive influence of computers has contributed to the widespread acceptance of data as the basis of thought. Before computers became the source of new metaphors, *data* were what economists, sociologists, and other social scientists gathered, studied, and generally misrepresented as objective. Within many circles of academia, data-based thinking was considered highly reductionist and definitely not on par with knowledge. In cultures that have been marginalized by the high-status knowledge promoted in universities, *wisdom* represents the highest and most valued form of knowledge. The rapid change in our language, which is reflected in the status differences now associated with *data, knowledge,* and *wisdom,* directly corresponds to changes in the stratification patterns of society—and, on a global scale, between cultures. Thus we must begin clarifying what the metaphors of the computer subculture illu-

minate and hide, and who gains and who loses from those metaphors that encode unrecognized cultural assumptions.

Specifically, I will argue that the metaphorical language, ideology,
and experience of computer-mediated thought reinforces a view of
individualism, language, temporality, moral relativism, and anthropocentrism that make it more difficult to recognize differences in
cultural ways of knowing. The double bind in how a culturally specific way of knowing makes its own assumptions increasingly difficult to recognize has implications more serious than the problem
of cultural domination. It also obscures the fact that our ecological
crisis is essentially a crisis of cultural beliefs and values. The way of
thinking reinforced by computers hides the cultural roots of our
ecological crisis while promoting an eco-management mind-set that
relies on scientific and technological fixes rather than changes in cultural assumptions and values.

In chapter 3 I examine the ecological implications of displacing
local knowledge with data and simulations. While data and simulations are important to high-status forms of knowledge, local
knowledge (which has been designated by educational institutions
as low-status) is renewed through narratives, highly contextualized face-to-face interactions, mentoring, and elder relationships. I
look at the connections between a print-based mode of representation that computers promote and an abstract, decontextualized way
of thinking. Cultures primarily based on oral communication experience different forms of consciousness and patterns of interaction. Indeed, scholars such as Walter Ong (1982), Eric Havelock
(1986), and Keith Basso (1996) have pointed out that orality is an essential aspect of communities where reciprocity continues to be a
vital part of life. I also examine the argument that local knowledge
is important to living within the limits of natural systems, particularly as that argument relates to the cultural orientation reinforced
by computers.

In chapter 4 I examine the cultural issues raised by the ways technology proponents use evolutionary theory to explain the development and global spread of computers. The writings of Hans Moravec, Gregory Stock, and Kevin Kelly articulate the connection between computers and the part of evolutionary theory that foregrounds the fitness of organisms to successfully compete in their environment. What is important about their arguments is that cultures are represented as engaged in the same competitive struggle. Their use of this powerful scientific metanarrative has important implications that current discussions about computers ignore. First, they equate evolution with the Western myth of progress and thus use it to legitimate the spread of computers. Second, in reinforcing the assumption that nontechnologically oriented cultures must either adopt computers or become extinct, the theory of evolution frames the discussion so that differences in cultural forms of knowledge and intergenerational communication appear irrelevant. Third, the scientific metanarrative marginalizes the need to consider the long-term implications of displacing diverse cultural metanarratives, which form the basis of moral authority, with the instrumental and individualistic morality characteristic of cyberspace. Ironically, while computers mediate culturally specific ways of thinking and communicating, computer proponents rely on an explanatory framework that cannot address differences in cultural values and ways of knowing and how these differences relate to the ecological crisis.

Chapter 5 provides the theoretical basis for the reform proposals suggested in later chapters. The chapter includes an examination of how proponents of computer-based learning—from computers in the early grades to virtual universities—represent its apparent educational advantages. It focuses on the forms of learning that are marginalized, misrepresented, and entirely eliminated. For example, abundant evidence shows that the storage and reproduction characteristics of language have culturally specific influences on the learning process. Instead of adopting a cultural view of intelligence, the proponents of computer-based learning continue to base their arguments on the Cartesian view of intelligence as an attribute of the autonomous individual. Only by unveiling the pro–educational computing stance can we recognize how computers reproduce the patterns of thinking that coevolved with the Industrial Revolution and establish a stronger conceptual basis for determining appropriate uses of computers in the classroom.

In chapter 6 I argue (by focusing on educational software that is ecologically destructive and culturally insensitive) that the integral language processes that are a part of primary socialization reproduce ways of knowing deeply rooted in the past. Primarily because of their own inadequate university education, few teachers understand the power of cultural mediation inherent in computer-based learning and communicating and are unaware of their responsibilities for supplementing the educational limitations of this technology. For example, teachers seldom notice the cultural assumptions reproduced in educational software programs such as *SimLife* (which portrays students as rational engineers of natural systems) and *Dinosaur Park* (which has children deciding how to maximize profits in a theme park). Thus they miss opportunities to engage students in a deeper examination of our dominant culture's implicit assumptions. I also explain how computer-mediated learning is part of the primary socialization process, which requires a teacher's professional judgments if the process is to cultivate the student's communicative competence. This form of primary socialization reinforces in the student's thought patterns the same assumptions that the software programmers take for granted.

Chapter 7 highlights the collective insensitivity of professionals and experts to the cultural changes technology (particularly computers) causes. Such insensitivity reflects our educational institutions' failure to provide an in-depth, critical, and comparative examination of the technology's impact on different cultures and ecosystems. Ironically, while schools and universities promote areas of study that lead to rapid technological innovation, little attention is given to understanding how technology affects the quality of individual and community life. Nor do public schools and universities provide a forum for examining the ecological impact of the resulting transformation in cultural values and practices. This chapter presents reforms that could address such a forum, which is an essential component of a democracy.

I make these suggestions with full awareness that educators are allocating more of their resources to adding computers to classrooms and "delivering" university courses over the Internet. By presenting the arguments in earlier chapters, which explain how computers contribute to the globalization of ecologically destructive cultural patterns, my hope is that educators and the general public will reconsider the wisdom of this trend.

# 2 The Culture of Cyberspace and Everyday Life

The cost of participating in cyberspace—for individuals, corporations, and social institutions ranging from hospitals to universities—is high and climbing higher as the industry moves closer to realizing its vision of a ubiquitous and seamless web of information exchange. But the current and future losses connected with their experiment with the world's cultural foundations cannot be measured only monetarily. While future economic losses may be gauged by environmental degradation, each culture will apply its own values when judging the impact of cyberspace on its traditions.

The media occasionally portray economic losses connected with computer systems, such as the Internal Revenue Service's $50 million investment in PCs for its agents, which resulted in a 40 percent reduction in caseload processing. This was a success story compared to the $300 million the IRS invested in another computer system that could never be made to work and that cost an additional $13 million to pay off the contractor, which could not supply a workable system. The General Accounting Office has estimated that from 1993 to 1998 federal agencies and departments spent $145 billion on computers (not counting computers for weapons systems). The Department of Defense and the Department of Housing and Urban Development have been unable to account accurately for their budget allocations. Similar records of inflated promises and failed systems exist at state levels; these have added to computer company profits but have left state legislatures fewer resources for addressing educational and human service needs. For example, the State of Washington abandoned its multimillion dollar effort to computerize its Department of Motor Vehicles, and Oregon officials witnessed the budget triple for a similar computer system that continues to be unworkable.

These represent just a few examples that run counter to the steady diet of computer euphoria the media and computer industry feed the U.S. public. Even apparent gains in productivity, such as AT&T's ability to handle 50 percent more calls with 40 percent fewer operators, cannot be adequately measured by profit margins alone. The resultant loss of forty thousand workers affected thousands of personal lives and the quality of life in hundreds of communities.

There are other losses that cannot be measured solely by economics yet are absolutely essential to consider when judging the merits of cyberspace. Critics such as Theodore Roszak (1994), Hubert Dreyfus (1986), Jerry Mander (1977), Joseph Weizenbaum (1976), David Noble (1998), and Langdon Winner (1986) provide a more complex understanding of the culturally specific way of knowing privileged by computers and the changes that computers introduce into the life of the community. They frame their concerns, however, largely within Western cultural traditions and focus primarily on the dangers of overemphasizing computer-mediated forms of intelligence. While I agree with most of the arguments of this surprisingly small group of critics, I would like to look at computers in light of the impact of Western technological and consumer culture on the earth's ecosystems. Does the globalization of cyberspace contribute to the loss of cultural diversity and thus the loss of knowledge of sustainable living within local ecosystems? Television commercials from MCI and IBM, which portray computers as tools for overcoming the gender and racial biases that often accompany face-to-face communication and providing the problem-solving technology that Tibetan monks and Greek fishermen rely on, were attempting to show the public that networking ability supersedes the differences in cultural ways of knowing. The message is that computers create a common

culture and thus a common language that is not limited by generations of experience in a specific bioregion.

In considering the connection between computers, cultural diversity, and the ecological crisis, we should pay heed to the continuity between digitized cultural experience, which computer proponents now celebrate as the dawn of a new age of personal freedom,
and the Industrial Revolution. Such a connection contradicts the
view of history the computer industry is now perpetuating to create
inevitability in the public mind and to secure our buy-in. Instead of
being captivated by glowing futuristic perspectives, we should recognize how the destructive traits of a now seemingly irrelevant era
are being carried forward. One such trait is the globalization of
the market culture that was a prominent feature of the Industrial
Revolution.

Before assessing the ecological consequences of a globalized, computerized consumer society, I first would like to clarify the cultural
differences between cyberspace and face-to-face interactions, which
vary widely around the world. Sorting out these differences and similarities is essential to recognizing that cyberspace represents an experience that is not culturally neutral. The comparison clarifies how
the introduction of computers into other cultures undermines a cultural group's ability to maintain the integrity of its traditions and
avoid becoming technological satellites of the West. Sorting out the
differences also illustrates that computers cannot simulate everyday
life. It helps us clarify how the language used to explain cyberspace
limits critical reflection in the public understanding.

### Cyberspace As Explained to the Public

Since the introduction of the word *cyberspace* in William Gibson's
science fiction novel *Neuromancer* (1984), it has become a context-

free term for all forms of computer-mediated electronic coding. It now stands for e-mail, near instantaneous data transfers among corporations and governmental agencies, research in virtual libraries, the paintings in virtual art museums, and so forth. The range of problem solving and visualization of simulated realities in cyberspace are equally impressive—from designing buildings and airplanes to simulating biological processes.

Increasingly, cyberspace has come to represent a radically different form of existence in human history. Computer proponents write about entering a new utopia where the genius of technology frees individuals from the limitations of time and space, the norms of local culture, and even their own psychological and biological constraints. The current ability to digitize what previously required direct hearing, seeing, and touching, combined with the exponential increase in the speed of information processing, has led to virtual reality experiences that involve more complete physical and psychological immersion. Faster computer chips and more sophisticated software promise to expand even further the frontiers of cyberspace, while further marginalizing cultural activities that cannot be reduced to such simulations.

In her widely acclaimed book *Life on the Screen: Identity in the Age of the Internet* (1996a), Sherry Turkle gives a glowing account of how cyberspace provides the fullest realization of our potential as postmodern individuals. In addition to her prediction that the culture of simulation (cyberspace) will enable us to "think of ourselves as fluid, emergent, de-centered, multiplicitous, flexible, and ever in process" (pp. 263–264), she makes several other claims about how computers will change our lives. One of them is that people will become "increasingly comfortable with substituting representations of reality for the real" (p. 23). In commenting on how the experience of cyberspace has changed her own sense of reality, she notes that the "culture of simulation encourages me to take what I see on the screen at (inter)face value." She further adds that "in the culture of simulation if it works for you it has all the reality it needs" (p. 24).

Steven R. Holtzman (1994) and Michael Heim (1994) represent individual emancipation and personal transformation in cyberspace as even more promising and revolutionary. According to Holtzman,

> We will be able to explore and experience other worlds, other realities. Another planet. Alternatively, Earth in the year 200,000 B.C. You will look around and see dinosaurs. In fact, you are a dinosaur. There is no reason why, in this virtual world, you must maintain human form. Given our mapping of movements, your arms and legs become the legs of dinosaurs or the wings of pterodactyls.
>
> The reality does not need to correspond to any real existing world. It can be an imaginary world, a new world created for the first time. You can become the first explorer of this new world. Or the reality may be a different view of the world. (P. 207)

Heim's prediction is that future computer technology will enable individuals to move to a postsymbolic stage of thought and communication. One manifestation of this new state of consciousness will be a form of communication that goes "beyond verbal or body language to take on magical, alchemical properties." As the bind of a traditional cultural language limits Heim's vision of life in cyberspace, he can only hint at what the future holds. For example, "a virtual-world maker might conjure up hitherto unheard-of mixtures of sight, sound, and motion." He goes on to suggest that when "consciously constructed outside the grammar and syntax of language, these semaphores [will] defy the traditional logic of verbal and visual information" (1993, p. 116). These predictions have a Book of Revelations tone to them, which Heim later qualifies by suggesting that individuals will need to remain connected to the "real world." "To banish constraints," he warns, "might disqualify virtuality from having any degree of reality whatsoever." But even this attempt to re-establish what he calls a "reality anchor" is undermined by the greater potential of cyberspace. As he puts it, "cyberspace can contain many alternative worlds, but the alternateness of an alternate world resides in its capacity to evoke in us alternative thoughts and alternative feelings" (p. 137).

In a chapter titled "A Slice of Life in My Virtual Community," Howard Rheingold discusses another dimension of cyberspace that needs to be considered from an ecological and cultural perspective. His views come from years of participation in the WELL, a virtual community in the San Francisco Bay Area that became, like gardening on Sunday, a regular part of his daily life. Thus, he does not foreground the postmodern expressions of individual subjectivity that Turkle views as so promising. Rather, he lists the characteristics and qualities of virtual communities that he finds engaging, as well as questions about the differences between virtual and real (off-line) communities. Information exchanges, dialogues centered on mutual interest, on-line interactions with many participants, and the need to create reciprocity characterized by wit, linguistic elegance, and promptness are just a few of the benefits he finds in cyberspace. While the questions Rheingold raises about the differences between the two forms of community suggest a more grounded understanding noticeably absent in most discussions of cyberspace, his questions nevertheless ignore cultural differences in the patterns of community life. By ignoring these differences, it becomes easier to ignore the critically important questions that underlie the ecological differences between virtual and real communities. Rheingold does not consider how virtual communities reinforce the destructive patterns of cultures that have harmed the environment.

At first glance, the benefits that Rheingold presents are not arguable. But his discussion of community is too conventional to illuminate the patterns that computer-mediated thought and communication reinforce. If we are to understand the errors of representing cyberspace as a culturally neutral medium and the ways the technology deepens the crisis of a consumer lifestyle that exceeds the earth's sustaining capacity, we must examine more closely the cultural patterns reinforced in computer-mediated thought and communication.

## Cyberspace As a Cultural Experience

On one level cyberspace represents mathematically coded electronic impulses. On another level, it represents someone sitting in front of a screen, moving a cursor, and typing letters on a keyboard, engrossed in the reflective and imaginative process of manipulating images and interpreting the mix of on-screen symbols as a distinct cultural experience. The reduction of sound, visual images, and space to mathematical code represents a profoundly different cultural view of reality. The critical question is whether this view will enable the world's cultures to meet more adequately our growing need for protein, fiber, fresh water, and shelter. There is also the question of whether computers lead us to substitute decontextualized ways of thinking about the world for the sensory encounters with the natural world that intertwine our lives.

Before we can answer these vital questions, we must first examine the cultural mediating characteristics of computers. We see how computers reinforce or marginalize culturally specific patterns of thought and communication in how the technology encodes the cultural assumptions of those who design them. Unfortunately, users who share with creators the same cultural assumptions do not see this inherent bias. However, members of other cultures are aware that when they use computers they must adapt themselves to radically different patterns of thought and deep culturally bound ways of knowing. If they accept computers uncritically as a culturally neutral technology and as the latest expression of modern progress, they may not recognize how their interactions with computers are changing them.

As I am arguing here that technology, especially language-processing technologies, is not in itself culturally neutral, I will first clarify how I am using the word *culture*. The anthropologist Clifford Geertz (1973) provides perhaps the most elegant yet comprehensive definition: "The culture concept . . . denotes an historically transmitted pattern of meanings embodied in symbol systems of inherited conceptions expressed in symbolic forms by which men [and women] communicate, perpetuate, and develop their knowledge about and attitudes toward life" (p. 89). Ward Goodenough (1981) provides an even more succinct explanation. As he summarizes it, culture "consists of standards for deciding what is, standards for deciding what can be, deciding how one feels about it, standards for deciding what to do about it, and standards for deciding how to go about doing it" (p. 62).

Geertz's reference to "historically transmitted patterns of meaning" brings out a critically important aspect of language that software designers and computer industry public relations representatives ignore. The shared meanings, patterns, and norms of a cultural group—from metacommunication processes to architectural forms, from child-rearing practices to the distribution of wealth—are transmitted, renewed, and modified through language. As Goodenough puts it, "to learn the language—that is, to learn to use its vocabulary acceptably—is indispensable for learning the cultural forms the vocabulary encodes" (1981, p. 66).

As these definitions foreground the shared nature of cultural patterns, it is important to recognize the range of diversity within a cultural group, as well as a subculture's ability to adopt the assumptions of a dominant culture. The multilayered differentiation of cultural patterns reflects religious, ideological, rural, urban, regional, and even individual and biological differences. As I travel around North America, I am aware that people who call themselves Canadians do not share all the same patterns with others who also call themselves Canadians. The range of diversity is equally great when I travel from the West Coast of the United States to New England or the Southwest. Yet there are commonly held patterns that distinguish Canadians from Americans and that distinguish both these groups from the indigenous Central Americans or those from India and China. Any use of the word *culture* today must also include intercultural exchanges of patterns, technologies, and symbols. The English eat Indian curries; indigenous youth in Oaxaca wear Chicago Bulls jerseys; and U.S. manufacturers maintain Japanese-style "just in time" inventories: these examples of syncretism incorporate external cultural forms into a core set of beliefs and practices that in themselves are becoming more syncretistic in nature. Both Geertz and Goodenough recognize that few if any cultures today are immune to the significant influences of contact with other cultures. They are also highlighting that, even within the context of change, there is still a continuity of patterns over generations. Their view of the intergenerational nature of cultural patterns challenges the Western idea of individual autonomy. My use of the word *culture* in the context of distinguishing between modern and postmodern culture (or Western and traditional culture) can lead to misunderstandings if the reader assumes that I am regarding modern and traditional culture as monolithic. Like Geertz and Goodenough, I am attempting to foreground the dominant or core patterns—those that are most often associated with modern or traditional cultures. In spite of the power of modern communication, which crosses so many cultural boundaries, identifiable differences still exist between modern and traditional cultures—particularly in their ways of communicating, storing, and renewing symbolic knowledge. These qualifications— particularly how the linguistic processes that computers cannot accommodate strengthen the core patterns of modern culture while undermining traditional cultures—need to be kept in mind as we explore the cultural mediating characteristics of computers in the following pages.

While Goodenough refers to language in terms of the spoken and written word, if we think of language more broadly, then we must include the ways a culture reproduces its symbolically based norms, its ways of understanding relationships, and its material constructions. It further requires that we recognize that the most widely shared core of symbolic knowledge is rooted in mythopoetic narratives so ancient that the current generation may not recognize their origins. How many of us in the dominant culture, for example, understand why we privilege sight over our other senses, or what the origins are of the individualism that forms the basis of our experience of the world as objective observer and independent actor? These symbolic trace elements, in being re-enacted and affirmed in thought patterns of even the most reflective individuals within the dominant culture, suggest the need to understand culture as a symbolic ecology that extends beyond the memory of its individual members. That constitutive mythopoetic narratives (such as the Hopi account of Kokyangwuti [Spider Woman], the Book of Genesis, the Vedas of Hinduism, and so forth) encode a cultural group's earliest understanding of human-to-nature relationships is important to understanding the impact cultures currently have on natural systems—including the impact of a cultural lifestyle reinforced in cyberspace. Any discussion of the cultural characteristics of cyberspace must address the role that language plays in maintaining intergenerational continuity within a culture. Because modern thinkers generally view themselves as separate from the past, this continuity is often ignored.

The deeply layered metaphorical nature of language is particularly relevant to understanding computer-mediated cultural patterns of thought and communication. Friedrich Nietzsche's observation that we understand and name new dimensions of experience in terms of familiar analogues continually bears on daily experience, especially in the deliberate pursuit of high-status knowledge and innovation. The vocabulary that has coevolved with technological development (indeed, influenced its direction) is particularly rich in metaphorical thinking. Words such as *artificial intelligence, memory, data, architecture, hacker, flame, information highway, net,* and so forth borrow from a domain of familiar experience in order to provide a basis of understanding a new domain with an as-yet-unconventional naming process. Other metaphors, such as *virtual reality, cyborg,* and *virtual life,* have not been anchored in an analogue that the general public fully discerns and accepts.

This aspect of metaphorical thinking has long been common knowledge within certain sectors of the computer industry. However, several other aspects of the language/thought connection are not understood by the computer subculture, which includes software developers and writers such as Turkle and Negroponte. In order to represent accurately these less-understood aspects of metaphorical thinking, I first want to explain the nature and role of root metaphors in analogic thinking and in constituting the iconic metaphors so prevalent in everyday thought and discourse. I then would like to use the theory of metaphor to explain how cyberspace reinforces the same root metaphors that were the basis of the Industrial Revolution. Using a theory of metaphor as part of the analysis of the culture of cyberspace will also clarify how thinking about the social implications of computers, as well as how they are used to communicate, are based on a "conduit" view of language; that is, a view of language as a neutral medium for sending and receiving data, images, and ideas.

The root metaphors of a cultural group are based on its ancient mythopoetic narratives (or cosmology). Early Judeo-Christian teachings cultivate the assumption that the individual has a discrete spiritual identity; similarly, the Book of Genesis extolls the mythopoetic narrative that led to viewing men as dominant over both women and the environment. In terms of the mainstream Western culture that is the basis of the present-day materialist technological lifestyle, many of the formative root metaphors can be traced back to the transition from the medieval to modern view of reality. For example, the mechanistic view of life processes, the individualism that undergirds our basic social attitudes toward the external world, and the notion of change as the manifestation of progress represent root metaphors of a distinctly modern origin. The growing acceptance of the theory of evolution as a total explanatory framework, and thus a model of authoritative thinking, is an example of a root metaphor that is still developing. A root metaphor is distinctive in that it forms the basis of thinking and acting in many areas of cultural life. Patriarchy influenced our legal system, practice of medicine, philosophy, the arts, and so forth. Similarly, we have used the modern root metaphor of the industrial model of production in agriculture, forestry, education, city planning, and architecture. We can see the continuity of the mechanistic root metaphor from Johannes Kepler's explanation of the purpose of science to Francis Crick's explanation of the workings of neural networks and again to Hans Moravec's vision of computers replacing humans in the evolutionary process.

The most important characteristics of root metaphors include their original grounding in the mythopoetic narratives and powerful evocative experiences, and their self-perpetuating nature in the analogic thinking that occurs across the panorama of cultural experience. Root metaphors provide conceptual and moral coherence to a culture. They often go unnoticed because they are reproduced through linguistic processes that are mostly taken for granted.

As indicated earlier, analogic thinking involves comparing a new dimension of experience with something we already know. For example, the analogues of highways, communities, and rooms provide a schema that enables us to understand the computer version of an "information highway," "electronic community," "chat rooms," and so forth. Analogic thinking automatically highlights similarities and obscures differences—unless one intentionally points out differences and how they may be more significant than similarities. The hiding of differences between the analogue and the novelty reflects the way in which the prevailing, taken-for-granted root metaphors frame understanding and communication. In the examples just given, the deep cultural schema that represents change as linear and progressive leads to interpreting information highways and electronic communities as more progressive forms of experience. The implicit nature of root metaphors helps to marginalize the need to consider the differences.

I'd like to clarify another aspect of the metaphor-language relationship that is often ignored—even by scholars such as George Lakoff and Mark Johnson. Conventionally, metaphor is associated with analogic thinking; however, metaphors can also influence uses of language that do not involve thinking in analogies. Most of the words we string together into sentences are iconic (or image-based) metaphors. Examples of iconic metaphors include such words as *data, individualism, creativity, intelligence, community,* and so forth. If we examine the genealogy of these iconic metaphors we find that they carry forward the schema or template of understanding from an earlier process of analogic thinking. For example, the iconic metaphor of *individualism* during the Middle Ages meant to be a subject, which made sense within the symbolic framework that sustained and legitimated the feudal hierarchy. Currently, we associate individualism with the self-expression and freedom derived from the modern artist's reinvention of that earlier analogue. Similarly, *intelligence* is an iconic metaphor that encoded until recently what scientists and educators established earlier in the twentieth century as the analogue for individual, objectifiable intelligence. Basing their thinking on a different set of root metaphors, some scientists now suggest that most intelligence is genetically inherited. (In recent years ethnic groups have, understandably, challenged this analogue and its underlying root metaphors.)

When image words continue to reproduce the cultural pattern, schema, or explanation that prevailed over competing analogues, they help to organize our thought patterns in ways consistent with the new analogue. When the earlier analogue comes under scrutiny, the word may undergo a new phase of analogic meaning. It then becomes associated with the analogue that survives what is a highly political process. But the root metaphors constituted in the past continue to influence this redefinition process.

The following quotation from Francis Crick (1994) represents an example of how historically and culturally specific root metaphors continue to frame analogic thinking. It also illustrates how assumed iconic metaphors reproduce an image, schema, or definition derived from an earlier analogic process. The role that iconic metaphors play in the thought process (including Crick's own way of thinking) does not support his explanation of the brain—which ignores the connection between the metaphorical nature of language and culturally specific ways of knowing. In other words, language thinks us as we think within, and at times beyond, its conceptual and metaphorical possibilities.

> There is no clear distinction in the brain between hardware and software, and attempts to foist such theories onto its operations have been unfortunate. The justification for such an approach is that, although the brain is highly parallel, it has some sort of serial mechanism (controlled by attention) on top of all the parallel operations, so that it may superficially appear to be somewhat like a computer at the higher levels of its operation—those far from the sensory imputs. (P. 180)

This statement is a clear example of analogic thinking, which explores the similarities (or, in this case, dissimilarities) between the brain and the computer. The iconic metaphors seem taken for granted in Crick's thinking and are pervasive in his writing, appearing in almost every noun, verb, and descriptive adjective in this passage. For example, his reference to the operations and parallel processes of the brain, as well as to "sensory inputs," indicates a mechanistic influence on his understanding. While short examples such as this do not always reveal the influence of other root metaphors, the root metaphor of the individual as the basic social unit is clearly part of his way of thinking. In an earlier statement in his book *The Astonishing Hypothesis: The Scientific Search for the Soul* (1994), Crick states his central thesis as "you [the autonomous reader] are largely the behavior of a vast population of neurons" (p. 91).

As the example just given demonstrates, if Crick's readers share the same implicit root metaphors, they likely will not recognize the multiple layers of metaphorical thinking that Crick reproduces in his supposedly culturally unbiased explanations. However, if we ask whether his explanation would make sense to cultural groups that do not have a linear, progressive view of change; that do not think in the reductionist, materialist patterns of Western science; and that do not think of life processes as machinelike, it then becomes easier to recognize the culturally influenced nature of Crick's evolutionary and scientific explanation. Within the context of our own Western way of understanding, we can ask why Crick does not consider the influence of culture on the language and thought processes — especially since his mechanistic view is so clearly influenced by the deep metaphorical constructions of his language community. The use of nonmechanistic root metaphors has led to thinking of the brain and consciousness in very different ways. Witness Freud's theory of the unconscious and Bateson's argument that intelligence is a participatory process that involves the larger ecology of mind within which the individual exists.

I hope this brief explanation will help overcome the misconception of language as a conduit for ideas and data, or as a sender and receiver of communication—a view that dominates the discourse on how computers are improving the quality of our lives. I also hope this explanation will help overturn the misconception that metaphorical thinking only occurs in the liminal situations where the appropriate analogue is sought for understanding a new situation or idea. It should overturn yet another set of misconceptions about the individual's self-identity, subjective experience, and reflective and creative processes as free from the cultural influences reproduced through the metaphors that sustain everyday life, including the patterns re-enacted in cyberspace.

If this account of language as a carrier of culturally specific ways of knowing still appears irrelevant to a discussion of cyberspace, several examples from the writings of leading computer spokespersons may help establish that computer-mediated experience not only reinforces particular patterns of thinking but also legitimates a specific ideological orientation. In the chapter that Howard Rheingold contributed to the book *Global Networks: Computers and International Communication* (1993), he gives an account of one aspect of his experience in cyberspace:

> On top of the technology-imposed constraints, we who populate cyberspace deliberately experiment with fracturing traditional notions of identity by living multiple simultaneous personae in different virtual neighborhoods. We reduce and encode our identities as words on a screen, decode and unpack the identities of others. The way we use these words, in stories (true and false) we tell about ourselves (or about the identities we want people to believe us to be), is what determines our identities in cyberspace. (P. 61)

The cultural schema reproduced in this account of his cyberspace experience is largely taken for granted by members of the dominant, high-status culture in the West. The replacement of the traditional face-to-face formation of identity with the context-free, highly sub-jective and experimental identity is only imaginable in cultures that interpret change and experimentation as expressions of progress. Furthermore, only a culture that regards the individual as autono-mous can propagate a view of individual reality within a context free from social accountability, much less accountability to the "off-line" biotic community that sustains individual life. Rheingold's accept-ance of machine-mediated relationships also requires an assumed cultural schema that has lost touch with the communal memory that, in many cultures, carries forward the wisdom of fundamental relationships gleaned from centuries of interspecies communica-tion. Any discussion of the apparent freedoms of cyberspace must acknowledge that cultures around the world, such as the indigenous cultures in Central and South America and cultures in China, India, Southeast Asia, and Africa, are experiencing the consequences of de-graded natural systems.

The contrast between Rheingold's celebration of cyberspace re-lationships and the insights that John Berger gained from living with a group of peasants in rural France is particularly relevant here. Berger noted that the conservatism of the peasant lifestyle was rooted in a deep awareness that scarcity, given the unpredictability of envi-ronmental conditions, is an ever-present possibility. Reflecting on the assumptions about progress in modern ideologies and by people living in modern, urban settings, Berger concluded that the expe-rimentally based lifestyle thrives on the false cultural premise that progress does not depend on the contingencies of natural systems. Rheingold's account of cyberspace community reflects the afflu-ent, progressive, and experimental mind-set that fuels this cultural assumption.

But he is not alone in holding this view. Michael Benedikt, editor of *Cyberspace: First Steps* (1992), expresses this experimental, pro-gressive, and environmentally disconnected way of thinking when he writes that "in patently unreal and artificial realities . . . the principles of ordinary space and time can be violated with impunity. . . . And after all, why have cyberspace if we cannot (apparently) bend nature's rules there?" (p. 128). We find the same root metaphors of anthropocentrism, progress, and autonomous individualism in how Turkle (1996a) and Negroponte (1995) explain the educational advantages of cyberspace. In commenting on two popular educational software programs, *SimCity* and *SimEarth,* Turkle states that their purpose is for the student "to build a community, an ecosystem, or a public policy. The goal is to make a successful whole from complex, interrelated parts" (p. 149). The same cultural mind-set that represents humans as existing in an experimental relationship with natural systems is reproduced in the observation that "since computer simulation of just about anything is now possible, one need not learn about a frog by dissecting it." Negroponte goes on to suggest that "children can be asked to *design* frogs, to *build* an animal with frog-like behavior, to *modify* that behavior, to simulate the muscles, to *play* with the frog" (1995, p. 199, italics added).

To restate the basic issue: explanations of cyberspace are rooted in culturally specific metaphors that provide the schemata both for analogic thinking and for the iconic metaphors that perpetuate that thinking. Past discussions of technology represented its characteristics and human benefits only generally and obscured the deeply encoded metaphorical basis of knowing and values that fostered its development. As the current discourse surrounding computers, including the design processes ranging from microchips to software programs, continues this tradition, I would like to focus attention on how the actual experience of computer-mediated thought and communication (that is, the phenomenology of cyberspace) reinforces the thought patterns, values, and subjectivity that were also the basis of the Industrial Revolution. This will partly illuminate the difference between cyberspace culture and cultures in the nonelectronically mediated world. It will also provide a framework for under-standing the ecological implications of undermining traditional knowledge with the myth that "data" are the new source of empow-erment and human progress.

## Subjectivity in Cyberspace

The experience of self varies from culture to culture. The personal pronoun *I,* which is such a prominent characteristic of the thought and communication among Euro–North Americans, does not exist in other cultural language systems. Instead of experiencing inter-actions with the surrounding environment from a personal perspec-tive, which we express when we say "I see," "I want," and so forth, the experience of self in many non-Western cultures is more in-fluenced by ongoing relationships. Indeed, in some cultures a per-son's name reflects her or his standing in the family, such as second brother or first sister. Just as these language environments sustain a cultural sense of identity, the language environment of cyberspace plays a similar constitutive role. The technology influences which as-pects of personal experience will be amplified and which will be re-pressed or unrealized.

With the exception of the near-total immersion of virtual real-ity, the experience of self-other relationships in cyberspace ampli-fies the culture of autonomous individualism in various ways. The words, graphics, and images on the screen represent decontextual-ized forms of text that require individual interpretation and analysis. They require the use of sight as the medium of contact and reaction. The subjective experience of observing and reflecting on something that appears on the screen as objective, distant, and separate from self is very different, as Walter Ong informs us, from orally based in-teractions, in which memory and the five senses attune themselves to the context of the experience and which involve physical and mental participation in the reciprocal patterns of ongoing community life. Printed language, as opposed to oral language, further reinforces the authority of individual perspective first introduced by fifteenth-century Italian artists and, as mentioned earlier, is now integral to subjectivity that most North Americans take for granted.

There is another form of reductionism (or loss) connected with the print-based consciousness and social relationships reinforced in cyberspace. Sensory communication through the Internet, or modeling changes in a natural system, is limited to the visual encounter with what appears on the screen. The symbols or text must be read. Aside from current efforts to engineer voice-activated computers, and the suggestion of Rosalind W. Picard (1997) that computers be designed to recognize and respond to the emotions of the user, computers are part of a tradition of technology dependent on print-based communication. This tradition of technology has been limited in its ability to reproduce the embodied, sensory forms of knowing resulting from direct, nontechnologically mediated experience. As David Abram (1996) states,

> Only when we slip beneath the exclusively human (abstract) logic continually imposed upon the earth do we catch sight of this other, older logic at work in the world. Only as we come close to our senses and begin to trust, once again, the nuanced intelligence of our sensing bodies, do we begin to notice and respond to the subtle logos of the land. . . . The senses . . . are the primary way that the earth has of informing our thoughts and guiding our actions. Huge centralized programs, global initiatives, and other "top down" solutions will never suffice to restore and protect the health of the animate earth. *For it is only at the scale of our direct, sensory interactions with the land around us that we can appropriately notice and respond to the immediate needs of the living world.* (P. 268, emphasis added)

The sensory experience that virtual reality systems promise to restore will always be superficial renderings of the complex cultural patterns, sensory intelligence, and variegated rhythms of the natural world. They will be little more than sanitized versions of Disney theme parks that are designed to elicit predetermined sensory responses. The operative words in Abram's statement, "appropriately notice and respond to," indicate that genuine sensory experience cannot be preprogrammed and predecided without a direct physical relationship with the environment.

While we cannot avoid bringing either our unconscious, culturally biased thinking or our explicit expectations and interests to our experience of cyberspace, our reliance on decontextualized data as the basis of our thinking further strengthens our sense of rational, autonomous individualism. Manipulating data, typing a message on a keyboard, and searching through web sites are essentially solitary activities, even when collaborating with colleagues over the Internet. Our sense of subjectivity further alters how we experience the flow of time. While we now, through technology, can participate in past events as a listener and observer, we are still reinforcing our autonomous individualism when deciding which aspects of the past to activate electronically or when to turn off the computer in order to attend to other personal matters. Deciding what has authority continues to be a subjective matter, which is profoundly different from cultures where traditions have authority to guide present thought and behavior. Participating in cyberspace also involves individual judgment about our experience of time—how much we will allocate to a particular task or form of involvement, when we will experience the simulations, and even how we eliminate the more traditional limits of time on communication and problem solving. This temporal aspect of subjectivity carries over in how we experience change as a matter of personal control.

Computer-mediated thought and communication amplifies several other characteristics of individual subjectivity. Unlike the subjectivity in ecologically centered cultures, where the self is integral to a larger moral/spiritual ecology that includes other forms of life and creates strict norms governing reciprocal relationships, the subjectivity reinforced in cyberspace is anthropocentric. Humans can view the environment from a variety of self-interested perspectives: as a natural resource, as an object of natural beauty, as an engineering challenge in improving natural systems, as a source of leisure, and so forth. With varying degrees of realism, cyberspace accommodates all of these perspectives. But the mediation process cannot be altered to eliminate anthropocentrism from the subjectivity intrinsic to cyberspace. If the natural environment is represented on screen as a simulation, or as a technical problem to be solved, it is inherently understood from a technocentric perspective.

This individualistic and anthropocentric way of thinking is partly the result of the culturally influenced interpretative framework the individual brings to the computer. It is also attributable to how language in cyberspace frames and reproduces instrumental moral relationships, including the relationship between humans and nature. While the industry's explanation of computer-mediated thought represents language in cyberspace as the linkage in a sender-receiver model of communication, cyberspace's coding and reproduction patterns actually have more to do with how relationships are to be understood.

When we recognize that language reproduces a cultural group's understanding of relationships, which can be seen in its root metaphors and patterns of metacommunication, it becomes easier to understand how language also provides the moral codes that govern how relationships are to be understood and acted out. Language names the attributes of the other (such as plants, workers, social space, and so forth), the nature of our relationships to the other, and thus the moral templates for our actions in regard to the other.

The metacommunication that gives face-to-face communication its complexity of nuances and their intended implicit effect represents another area in which language clarifies our understanding of relationships. As with the language that established the basic differences in attributes that represented women as inferior to men and thus normalized inequitable treatment as morally appropriate, the language of computer-mediated thought and communication reproduces how a cultural group understands certain attributes, how we relate to these attributes, and what constitutes the moral norms governing the relationships. The sender-receiver model of communication, as well as the appearance on the screen of seemingly objective statements, data, graphics, and simulations, contributes to reinforcing an instrumental view of moral relationships. This moral orientation reinforces the anthropocentrism that characterized the early and more recent stages of the Industrial Revolution, from the early worldwide search for natural resources to the commodification process that is still part of contemporary computer-based eco-management projects.

For example, in *Wisdom Sits in Places: Landscape and Language Among the Western Apache* (1996), Keith H. Basso describes how the Western Apache of the Cibecue region of Arizona use the place names of the local geography to encode ancient wisdom about moral relationships and qualities of character. Thus, the name of a water hole, location of a grove of cottonwoods, and an outcropping of white rock serve as reminders of the first storied experiences of the ancestors. In learning the names given to the landscape and the accompanying stories, the young Western Apaches are learning the ancient moral insights that are to guide them in their relationships with each other and to the land.

Basso describes the form of subjectivity that accepts guidance from the wisdom of ancestors and the moral lessons encoded in the place names in the following way:

As conceived by Apaches from Cibecue, the past is a well-worn "path" or "trail" (*'intin*) which was traveled first by the people's founding ancestors and which subsequent generations of Apaches have traveled ever since. Beyond the memories of living persons, this path is no longer visible—the past has disappeared—and thus it is unavailable for direct consultation and study. For this reason, the past must be constructed—which is to say, imagined—with the aid of historical materials, sometimes called footprints or tracks . . . that have survived into the present. These materials come in various forms, including Apache place-names. (P. 31)

This way of understanding relationships, according to Basso, is based on a spatial rather than individual view of moral authority. In commenting on how widely this form of subjectivity was shared among indigenous cultures of North America, Basso notes,

For Indian men and women, the past lies embedded in the features of the earth—in canyons and lakes, mountains and arroyos, rocks and vacant fields—which together endow their lands with multiple forms of significance that reach into their lives and shape the way they think. Knowledge of places is therefore closely linked to knowledge of self, to grasping one's position in the larger scheme of things, including one's own community, and to securing a confident sense of who one is as a person. (P. 34)

Compare this radically different way of knowing and experiencing relationships with the previous description of cyberspace, how it reinforces a view of temporality that represents the individual sitting in front of a screen as having the ultimate authority for judging whether the past is relevant to the present and how it is to be interpreted.

Another critically important characteristic for understanding the cultural influence of cyberspace also had its origins in the earliest stages of the Industrial Revolution. Among the Industrial Revolution's many cultural changes, one of the most important was the transformation of the market from a place of economic exchange within the community to a universal principle encompassing all forms of human activity, relationships, and knowledge. The extension of the market principle, where the logic of supply, demand, and profits determines which aspects of community life can be commodified and marketed globally, continues today as one of the primary goals of the computer industry. Indeed, a successful corporation is one that can turn a form of face-to-face relationship or a mental or physical task into a new niche market for computer-based technologies. While Turkle (1996a, 1996b), Negroponte (1995), Papert (1980), and other proponents focus our attention on the marvels of computer technologies, we must keep in mind that computer technology represents the digital phase of the Industrial Revolution; that is, it perpetuates the primary goal of transforming more aspects of everyday life into commodities that can be manufactured and sold, now on a global basis.

This connection between computers and the economic and technological dynamic of commodification is highly relevant to understanding how computer-mediated thought and communication reinforce a culturally biased form of subjectivity. As children participate in computer-mediated experiences, from games to problem solving simulations, they are learning, as part of their natural attitude toward themselves and others, to be consumers of the latest computer technology. Their natural attitude, which is an expression of a culturally specific form of subjectivity, is thus being shaped by economic and technological forces that require a continual escalation in what is expected of the normal and successful person. Seymour Papert summed up the drive to make humans dependent upon computers in every aspect of individual and communal experience when he responded to a reporter's question by saying, "Our goal in education is to foster the ability to use the computer in everything we do" (Evenson, 1997, p. 3). By shaping consciousness and bodily experience to accept computer mediation as normal, the computer subculture (which is fast becoming the dominant culture) is also defining what is abnormal, deviant, and deficient.

Just as computer literacy frames computer illiteracy as socially abnormal and deficient, the individuals and cultural groups that do not participate fully in the seamless web of cyberspace are increasingly framed as less developed and thus less intelligent. What both critics and promoters of computer technology are overlooking is the fact that "normality" today involves certain consequences, one of which is the further commodification of individual and community experience. As we witness the signs of apparent progress in other cultures, marked by the growing use of computers and other Western products, we are also witnessing the emergence of Western individualism and subjectivity. And because we view the Western lifestyle as a positive development, we tend to ignore how the historically grounded and culturally specific expressions of subjectivity now being displaced by computers contribute to meaningful community life and to sustainable ecosystemic relationships.

## Cyberspace and the Real World

To summarize the previous section, the subjectivity of cyberspace expresses all the attributes of the individualism of the Industrial Revolution: a natural attitude toward being a rational, self-determining individual who looks on both past and future in terms of immediate self-interest; a view of the environment as a technological and economic opportunity; an expectation that change leads to a personal enlargement of material well-being; and a view of the world's other cultures as evolving toward the rootless individualism that can easily adapt to the rapidly changing routines of technologically intensive modes of production.

Noticeably absent from the current discussion of the social implications of computers is the recognition that only a small minority of the world's population subscribes to the type of individualism reinforced in cyberspace. More importantly, the cultural patterns the individualist takes for granted are profoundly different from the patterns taken for granted by other cultural groups. A consideration of these differences should lead computer proponents to be more cautious about representing cyberspace as the next evolutionary stage of global cultural development. Building on the writings of the Chinese psychological anthropologist Francis L. K. Hsu, Ron Scollon and Suzie Wong Scollon observe that "unlike the Euro-American view that represents the individual as the basic social unit, with the biological self providing the boundary between self and the Other, the Chinese concept of the person places the major boundary that separates self from Other beyond the family unit. . . . [S]uch relationships as those with one's parents and children are considered inseparable aspects of the self" (1992, p. 9). The Scollons' fieldwork with the Koyukon of Central Alaska provides a glimpse of yet another view of individualism—one that is shared by other Athabaskan cultural groups spread across North America. In addition to using language that frames actions as reciprocal relationships, the Scollons found that "the Athabaskan sense of self seems to carry with it no requirement to express itself to others nor, perhaps, to oneself. What can be said with certainty . . . is that Athabaskans guard the sense of self in situations where communication might be problematical through exercising a great deal of care over the amount of talk they are willing to use" (p. 21). The natural attitude toward quietness, as opposed to filling time and space with talk, reflects a sense of self that is particularly at odds with the acceleration of communication that computers are designed to facilitate.

The linear view of time amplified in cyberspace, where individual autonomy puts both the past and the future on equally subjective footing, is radically different from the cyclical view of time many cultures use to organize life processes. In addition, the assumption that the brain and other organic and cultural processes are machinelike and thus capable of being re-engineered differs fundamentally from the metanarratives of cultures that represent human and nonhuman forms of life as participants in the same moral and spiritual universe. This deep sense of sacred unity and interdependency, which is especially visible in cultures that have complex systems for honoring and renewing the reciprocal relationships between humans and the greater biota, is totally absent from culture of cyberspace. Recent efforts to establish spiritual sites on the Internet have the same superficiality that characterizes electronic communities.

It would be easy to cite other fundamental differences in the deep symbolic foundations of cultural groups, but something more needs to be said about the differences between computer-mediated and face-to-face communication. Media announcements and industry hype about entering the digital phase of human evolution ignore a fundamental characteristic of everyday reality: namely, that everyday life involves face-to-face interaction. These interactions, whether they occur in the home, between neighbors, on the sidewalk, in the workplace, or at a musical event, involve the communication of personal attitudes toward the other in culturally patterned ways. Ideas, requests, conversations about matters of mutual interest, and so forth are communicated as part of a larger cultural ecology of interaction. This complex and highly fragile process of framing mutual focus and relevance enables face-to-face communication to be meaningful and establishes the culturally prescribed status relationship between the communicators. Tone of voice, gaze, pattern of touching, and content of verbal response are just a few of the metamessages that signal how the participants are experiencing and judging relationships. The expression of patterns that communicate what the relationship is, and the acceptance by the other of what these patterns signify, allows certain things to be said that would be considered inappropriate in a different status relationship. For example, the stranger who uses the other person's first name, touches the other's arm while speaking, and reveals what normally would be considered intimate experience is attempting to establish a footing that will likely be rejected—which the other signifies by attempting to separate as quickly as possible.

Footing and framing, cultural patterns that regulate the dynamics of conversational turn-taking—including the constant need to balance solidarity and power—are just a few of the dimensions of face-to-face communication that require the use of paralinguistic cues, body language, and space as part of a metacommunication process. Metacommunication involves the expression of both personal preferences and ideas and culturally shared patterns of communication, most of which are learned in context and at a implicit level of awareness. Metacommunication is an indirect form of communication about a relationship that may explicitly involve an exchange of information, the sharing of a personal insight or greeting, and so forth. While different cultural groups may share certain patterns of metacommunication, other patterns that are taken for granted within a cultural group may not even be recognized by an outsider, much less understood. Because metacommunication is learned tacitly and in context, it is integral to face-to-face communication but not to print-based communication—which means it is not part of the culture of cyberspace.

The inability of cyberspace to accommodate the multiple layers of meaning and messages that are part of face-to-face communication has important implications for the formation of a person's sense of identity. To illustrate, I'd like to point out the connection Alasdair MacIntyre (1984) draws between self-identity and narratives of the community:

> The other aspect of narrative selfhood is correlative: I am not only accountable, I am one who can always ask others for an account,

who can put others to the question. I am part of their story, as
they are part of mine. The narrative of any one life is part of an
interlocking set of narratives. Moreover, this asking for and giving
of accounts itself plays an important part in constituting narratives. (P. 218)

Compare this view—that participating in the interlocking narratives of community shapes individual identity and sustains community life—with Turkle and Rheingold's views of self-identity in
cyberspace and with the increasingly popular approach to digital
storytelling. Promoters of cyberspace communities claim that computers allow for stories with multiple plot lines that can be shared
with a worldwide audience. They further claim that computer-
mediated narratives and stories about actual or imaginatively constructed events allow for interactive relationships that duplicate the
experience of community—but on a scale not limited by the temporal and spatial boundaries of geographical communities. Our desire to share stories is a deep human need to be part of the web of interdependent relationships that constitute community. To try to fill
that need in cyberspace, where there are no shared memories, moral
responsibilities, or even known identities, is profoundly different.
The limitations of substituting the decontextualized realm of cyberspace for culturally grounded narratives and storytelling are clearly
evident in how Turkle and Rheingold think about community.

In recalling Turkle's views on the constructed nature of reality and
self-identity, it is important to recognize that she considers "one's
story" as emerging from "thinking of ourselves as fluid, emergent,
decentralized, multiplicitous, flexible, and ever in process" (1996a,
p. 263). It is not a story constituted within the framework of intergenerational narratives that characterize real communities. Her
description of the identity reinforced in cyberspace is that of supposedly autonomous individuals whose moral compass reflects the
constantly shifting subjective moods and experimentation in how

they want to represent themselves on the screen to others. To repeat a quote by Rheingold (1993) cited earlier, "On top of the technology-imposed constraints, we who populate cyberspace deliberately experiment with fracturing traditional notions of identity by living as multiple simultaneous personae in different virtual neighborhoods" (p. 61). In other words, the electronic "community" is populated by individuals who are free both of the moral constraints and the wisdom contained in the intergenerational narratives of the cultural group.

There are important political and moral implications in how cyberspace facilitates communication between individuals who share similar interests. At first glance, the ease of communication appears as a genuine gain. But these virtual communities of shared interests can also be understood as enclaves. According to Robert D. Putnam, the author of *Making Democracy Work* (1993), these enclaves are based upon horizontal networks of interpersonal communication that involve participants of electronically equivalent status, interest, and power. His research into the connections between networks, civic engagement, and democracy in Northern Italy led him to conclude that vertical networks of civic interaction (involving people from different social strata and with different interests, experiences, and cultural traditions) are essential to a democratic polity. "The denser such networks in a community," he observed, "the more likely that its citizens will be able to cooperate for mutual benefit" (p. 173). Learning the moral norms governing reciprocity in cyberspace, where participants may be representing themselves to others in highly experimental ways, is profoundly different from learning the moral norms that govern both the explicit and metacommunication patterns of face-to-face interactions in a culturally diverse community. This difference raises the question of whether access to more data facilitates democratic decision making, or whether democracy has more to do with learning the norms of reciprocity that are the basis of trust and mutual responsibility in a more diverse, face-to-face community. In *Democracy and Technology* (1995), Richard Sclove makes the following observation about the double bind of democratizing information through electronically mediated communication:

> No matter with whom one communicates nor how far one's imagination flies, one's body—and hence many material interdependencies with other people—always remains locally situated. Thus it seems morally hazardous to envision communicating with far-flung telemates, if that means growing indifference to physical neighbors. It is not encouraging to observe just such indifference in California's Silicon Valley, one of the world's most "highly wired" regions. (P. 80)

Just as data should be viewed as a degraded form of knowledge, computer-mediated communication should be viewed as a degraded form of symbolic interaction—one that reinforces the rootless individual who is comfortable with the expressions of self-creation that the computer industry finds profitable to encourage. We shall now examine how computers lead to the loss of local knowledge and the consequences of this loss for the environment and community self-sufficiency.

# 3 Displacing Wisdom with Data: Ecological Implications

At the fiftieth anniversary meeting of the Association of Computing Machinery held in 1997 in San Jose, California, leading contributors to computer development offered their views on the conference theme: "The Next Fifty Years of Computing." Joel Birnbaum, director of laboratories at Hewlett-Packard, prophesied that computer technology might advance to the point where people would wear an auxiliary brain that could instantaneously translate a foreign language as well as amplify the experience of the aesthetically sensitive person. Vinton Cerf, who helped pioneer the Internet, envisioned the routines of daily life—drawing our bath water, cooking our breakfast, monitoring the quality of our excretions—being organized by tiny computers. With only a few speakers expressing minor reservations, the consensus of opinion supported the prediction of Larry Ellison (president and CEO of Oracle): "By combining all information—numbers, texts, sound, and images—in digital form, and making it available everywhere, and by making it infinitely manipulable, the information highway will utterly change our lives." He further predicted that computers will so radically change our world in the next twenty years "that people will scarcely be able to remember what life was like before" (1994, p. 4).

In *The Road Ahead* (1995), Bill Gates is equally optimistic about the ability of computers to overcome any future problems that humankind might face. His optimism about the impact of computers is reflected in the following prediction:

[Computers] will enhance leisure time and enrich culture by expanding the distribution of information. It will relieve pressure on urban areas by enabling individuals to work from home or remote-site offices. It will relieve pressure on natural resources because an increasing number of products will be able to take the form of bits rather than of material goods. It will give us more control over our lives and allow experiences and products to be custom tailored to our interests. Citizens of the information society will enjoy new opportunities for productivity, learning, and entertainment. (P. 250)

What is extraordinary about how these industry leaders envision the future is that none of them mention the radically diverging trends between the world population growth and the quality of our environment. For an industry that represents itself as advancing humankind's ability to base decisions on vast amounts of instantly accessible data, they seem to be blind to the widely publicized data emerging from scientific studies of the human impact on natural systems. Contrary to the conference speakers' predictions, the data related to changes in natural systems, combined with the increase in world population and the consumer lifestyle, cannot be interpreted as evidence that the next fifty years will find the human situation transformed in the ways these computer futurists envision.

## Consumerism, Technology, and the Ecological Crisis

If we are to grasp the seriousness of this misunderstanding, we need a fuller account of the ecological crisis than that given in chapter 1. The essential data that should be considered when predicting the changes in human life over the next fifty years must be that associated with the rapid growth in world population. That growth, along with the spread of Western technology and consumerism, has led to critically important changes in Nature's life support systems. In calculating the level of consumption in various regions of the world, Mathis Wackernagel and William Rees (1996) note that the average "ecological footprint" in the United States is 5.1 hectares per person, while in India it is 0.4 hectares, and worldwide it is 1.9 hectares. (The ecological footprint represents the total amount of land required to produce energy, fiber, protein, and other life-supporting materials and to assimilate the waste products of consumption.) They further note that productive land has decreased on a worldwide basis from 5.6 hectares per person in 1900 to 1.5 hectares today. Wackernagel and Rees also state that if the entire world's population were to adopt the consumer lifestyle of the average North American "it would need two additional planets to produce the resources, absorb the wastes, and otherwise maintain life support" (p. 15).

More specific data may provide better insight into the degraded condition of natural systems that supply the basic necessities of human life, systems that took millions of years to reach the level of species diversity and complexity that are now threatened by mere decades of modern development. Topsoil loss, for example, is occurring much faster than topsoil formation, with approximately six million hectares of previously fertile land being abandoned each year. The increasing rate of deforestation is accompanied by an increase in the amount of carbon released into the atmosphere, which is estimated at nearly seven billion tons annually. This change in the carbon cycle, in turn, is contributing to global warming and to changes in weather systems—which are reflected in increasing financial losses to the insurance industry and to changes in agricultural productivity.

The seventeen world fisheries, which have been a major source of inexpensive protein for much of the world's population, are now in serious decline—with some fisheries in collapse. Fishing boats that can pull in a thirty-thousand-pound catch in a single pass of their trawl nets, and the 500,000 kilometers of nylon drift net set out daily six months of the year, are just two examples of how technology, greed, and extreme shortsightedness are undermining marine ecosystems just as human demands on them are rapidly increasing. The rate of deterioration led sixteen hundred marine biologists from around the world to sign a petition in 1999 urging that governments take immediate steps to protect the oceans from abuses of technology. Fresh water, which is essential for both drinking and agriculture, is in such short supply in many regions of the world (such as China, India, the American Southwest, Africa, and the Middle East) that the future water needs of urban areas can only be met by reducing the amount available for agriculture.

The state of the earth's ecosystems appear even more alarming when we consider the data on how the chemicals that form the basis of modern life are adversely affecting every aspect of the natural world: from coral reefs, bird populations, and harbor seals to cancer rates in humans. As Theo Colborn and others state in *Our Stolen Future* (1996), "With one hundred thousand chemicals in commerce globally and one thousand additional new substances coming onto the market each year, there is little hope of discovering their fate in ecosystems or their harm to humans until the damage is done" (p. 226). On the other hand, reactionary groups such as the Heritage Foundation, the Alabama Family Alliance, and Focus on the Family have all been trying to overturn the National Environmental Education Act and promote the view that the ecological crisis does not exist. The only problem, in their view, is that of liberals attempting to control people's lives.

Contrary to such views, which rely on a combination of nineteenth-century classical liberalism, populist conservatism, and the Internet, there is no evidence that ecosystems are recovering from the rapid decline we are now witnessing. Nor is there a basis for believing that the projected increase of the earth's human population over the next forty years will be accompanied by the continual rise in material well-being envisioned by Bill Gates, Larry Ellison, and other computer devotees.

Growth in worldwide trade, which continues to be a key measure of apparent economic progress, is simply another indicator of the commodification of more aspects of daily life. The vision upheld by Internet developers is that people living in remote areas will have instant access to the global electronic shopping mall, where a few keystrokes will provide access to London's Harrod's department store and other upscale on-line merchandise services. Computers also enable scientists to genetically alter local plant and animal life, which enables them to patent new gene lines and generate more products to market globally. For example, Monsanto, a major player in the development of genetically altered seeds, now markets Roundup Ready seeds for soybeans, canola, and corn and plans to market Roundup Ready sugar beets, wheat, and potatoes. (Roundup Ready seeds allow dangerous herbicides to be used more widely.) The increased variety of consumer products, combined with the ability to promote them in every home with a television and an Internet connection, helps to create illusions of plenitude and improved material well-being, and the sense that the only limitation of the present economic system is lack of money or credit to buy everything and be everything.

The advertising industry now depends on computers to enhance the images of successful, beautiful, happy people who are always represented as participating in some form of consumerism. Unfortunately, these images are often too seductive to be resisted by even the poorest of the poor. Witness the success of advertising campaigns in urban areas where there is high unemployment, low wages for those who find jobs, overcrowding, unsanitary housing, and high crime rates. The television commercials and other advertising are computer-generated in ways that integrate consumerism into popular themes of street culture. When our minds are focused on wearing clothes with high-status corporate logos, we are unlikely to be concerned about chemicals in our food, air, and drinking water. Nor are we likely to be aware that our food comes from ecosystems that have become less viable and thus less productive.

Computer industry leaders have amassed sufficient wealth (in some instances, excessive wealth) to insulate themselves from such environmental hazards. Their modes of travel and their destination points seldom bring them into contact with the effects of deforestation, depleted aquifers, and soil erosion (though they might find, coincidentally, that their favorite fishing streams have radically changed over the last few years). Their isolation from these effects accounts, in part, for their increasingly unrealistic and ecologically destructive vision of mediating more life experiences through cyberspace. It may be too much to expect them to reflect on whether their visions are ecologically sustainable, even for the short term. Changes in the modern ideal, which are increasingly centered on achieving a lifestyle of convenience and material well-being, will have to come from people who occupy the margins of the dominant culture and from the members of other cultures who can focus on the moral, spiritual, and even material losses associated with the growing electronic global village.

At some point the scientific studies of changes in natural systems, as well as media coverage of environmental disruptions, will lead us all to ask whether the technological approach to progress is a key part of the problem. As we are constantly reminded, computers now enable transnational corporations to lease their operations where wages, costs of materials and energy, and environmental regulation are the lowest. In many parts of the world (such as India, Africa, China, Central and South America, and Southeast Asia) people are openly resisting transnational corporations and the environmental destruction their activities bring about. The Chipko and Appiko movements in India, as well as the intensifying conflict in southern Mexico between indigenous cultures and the forces promoting technological development, are visible reminders that the Western approach to so-called progress is so devastating the environment that survival itself has become the dominant concern of many cultures in the Southern Hemisphere.

### Replacing Local Knowledge with Data

I present the following analysis of what is lost when local knowledge is displaced by the decontextualized and supposedly culture-free information communicated through cyberspace with the hope of clarifying how computers contribute to our global ecological crisis—and to the cultural domination against which many regions of the world are struggling.

In the following paragraphs I use the terms *data* and *information* to refer to the various forms of symbolic culture translated into the binary code of 1s and 0s and reproduced through the circuitry of a computer chip onto a computer screen or compact disc. As these words have become common among the members of society who most use computers and increasingly vague in their meaning, clarifying their usage is important.

As I pointed out in the previous chapter, to digitize thought and aesthetic expression is to abstract them from their multilayered cultural and ecological contexts. Like the printed word, the digital representation reinforces an entirely different form of consciousness and quality of interaction than what occurs in most face-to-face communication. At times, of course, face-to-face communication can be reduced to the exchange of abstract information or even data in its traditional sense.

The following changes seem especially important to consider: the increasing status accorded to technologically mediated data; how this form of knowledge undermines the importance and existence of local knowledge; and how the displacement of local knowledge with data and other decontextualized, electronically communicated symbol systems contributes to the consumer lifestyle that harms the environment.

First let's consider the ideological characteristics of data as a form of high-status knowledge. This will provide a basis for understanding why our educational institutions tend to ignore local knowledge and why our educational establishment trivializes efforts to learn from cultures that have avoided the technological approach to development.

If we use the word *ideology,* as Clifford Geertz (1973) suggests— to refer to a culturally based interpretative framework that influences how we think, value, perceive, and manipulate the world—it is easy to recognize the connections between data as high-status knowledge and the ideology of elite groups who promote technologically based economic development. Statements quoted earlier by Turkle (1996a, 1996b), Rheingold (1991, 1993), Ellison (1994), Gates (1995), and others reflect the key assumptions underlying the ideology of modern liberalism. They share a common way of interpreting individualism, the nature of change, the basis of moral authority, and human-to-nature relationships. Their interpretative framework (or ideology) is the same one that underlies the vision and self-justification of transnational corporations that perpetuate global development, which undermines the viability of natural systems and the self-sufficiency of indigenous cultures.

This ideology is also promoted through traditional academic disciplines and schools of professional study, such as business, education, journalism, and computer science. Indeed, because common assumptions about individualism, the progressive nature of change, the authority of abstract systems of representation, and so forth are taken for granted, their historical and cultural origins are ignored;

thus the ideology is easily universalized as the model that all cultures should imitate. This helps to justify its spread to other cultures through technological, economic, and educational means. Higher education, as Ivan Illich points out in *Deschooling Society* (1970), legitimizes the myth that "scientifically produced commodities" represent the highest measure of human achievement. As he puts it, the modern educational system "is simultaneously the repository of the society's myths, the institutionalization of the myth's contradictions, and the locus of the ritual which reproduces and veils the disparities between myth and reality" (p. 37).

The different dimensions of the myth are reflected in the key assumptions identified earlier, including the assumptions that intelligence is an individual attribute and that scientifically based forms of expert knowledge should guide the thought and actions of individuals. One contradiction inherent in the myth is that the curriculum of higher education, which includes such diverse areas as philosophy, economics, education, and psychology, contributes to the moral and material well-being of humanity. The reality, as the study of the declining condition of ecosystems shows, is that the values and forms of knowledge learned in universities contribute to the spread of consumerism, to the loss of knowledge that focuses more on relationships than economics, and to the acceleration of environmental decline. These disparities are hidden amidst the increasing numbers of university courses that include an environmental focus while reinforcing the cultural assumptions at the root of the Industrial Revolution.

The truth of these generalizations speaks for itself in that the typical university graduate does not recognize that the consumer lifestyle is ecologically unsustainable. The few who do recognize the double bind of consumerism face the challenge of freeing themselves from the academically reinforced myths that most university graduates still hold. A second manifestation of these generalizations is the inability of computer and technology experts to recognize different cultural ways of knowing, and that cultures that are not technologically oriented may have greater symbolic complexity and sophistication in other areas. Third, most university graduates do not understand the difference between high-status and low-status knowledge, the cultural forces at the root of this distinction, and the ways in which low-status, noncommodified knowledge enhances community life.

It is important to identify the characteristics of an educational ideology that would support local knowledge and traditions as a viable alternative to the current dominant models of development. Such an investigation is relevant for examining the ecological and communal consequences of displacing local knowledge with computer-mediated data and information.

As I have discussed these characteristics elsewhere (Bowers 1995, 1997), I shall summarize here only the main principles. The name that best describes this guiding interpretative moral framework is *cultural bioconservatism.* This awkward term has the virtue of representing culture as inseparable from its impact on natural systems and suggests the transformations that must occur if we are to separate ourselves from the deep and still unconscious legacy of the Industrial Revolution. By combining culture, the biotic community, and conservatism, the term acknowledges that cultural development should reflect the characteristics of the ecosystem that sustains it. Further, its moral orientation diverges from one of the main assumptions of modern liberalism: that change is inherently progressive. Instead of debating the effects of governmental actions on the environment, adherents of liberal thought debated which approach to technological and economic development and which form of expert knowledge would best facilitate change. (Even Marxist thinkers shared this assumption.)

Rather than assuming that experimentation with the conceptual and moral foundations of culture is essential to social progress, cultural bioconservatism is oriented toward conserving and renewing traditions that have proven over time to contribute to a community of morally reciprocal relationships and to the viability of local ecosystems. Unlike liberal traditions, this orientation has no guarantees based in taken-for-granted myths; instead, it considers the possibility of unanticipated natural occurrences that may imperil the survival of the community. Unlike most university graduates who think of traditions in terms of holidays or as a static cultural form that impedes the forward march of progress and individual freedom, cultural bioconservatism recognizes that traditions are neither static nor self-perpetuating. It further recognizes that some traditions were wrongly constituted in the first place, that others change too slowly, and that some traditions may be lost before members of the culture recognize their importance and hard-won history. The breakdown in the distinction between our private and public lives, which now turns our personal preferences and behaviors into marketable commodities, is an example of the latter.

Another key element of cultural bioconservatism includes the recognition that the individual is not autonomous and self-directing but is better understood as possessing a self-identity, a way of knowing and valuing, and a set of culturally influenced behavioral patterns that are reproduced through the everyday use of language. This view of the individual as a cultural being with a culturally rooted intelligence, creativity, and morality is best expressed in ways that take account of how the natural environment shapes and determines culture. As stated earlier, thinking of the individual as nested in culture, and culture as nested in natural systems, summarizes elegantly the fundamental dependencies and relationships cultural bioconservatism encompasses.

Like all metaphorical systems of understanding, ideology simultaneously illuminates and hides. Cultural bioconservatism provides the interpretative framework for recognizing local contexts, continuities of patterns, interdependencies, and consequences resulting from actions. It also presents a long-term perspective that brings the distant past and future into present-time decision making. Members of cultures that still have a cultural bioconservative ideology would view the tenets of modern liberalism—its ways of transforming knowledge into universally applicable abstract symbolic systems; its view of the individual as possessing ultimate rational and moral authority; and its emphasis on transforming skills, knowledge, and relationships into commodities—as intellectually and morally problematic. Similarly, the modern ideologies ranging from Libertarianism to Marxism (to identify the extremes) historically have been unable to recognize any merit in non-Western cultural ways of knowing. "If it is not modern, then it must be backward" has been the formulaic response of modern liberal ideologues. They have a similar record of dismissing ecologically centered beliefs and rituals that foster self-limitation for the sake of future generations and other forms of life. Nor have they been able to reconcile the value of renewing traditions with their continual quest for new and more powerful technologies and forms of critical expression. One of the ironies of their way of thinking is that they do not recognize that their antitradition stance is itself a long-standing tradition that extends back to European Enlightenment thinkers.

Given the diversity of cultural ways of knowing, and even the diversity of local knowledge within the dominant culture, the following discussion of local knowledge should not be interpreted as suggesting that all forms of local knowledge incorporate wisdom about how to live in nondestructive relationships with the environment. I am not suggesting that all forms of local knowledge meet our tacit moral standards of fairness and equity. The argument here is that environmentally sustainable expressions of local knowledge share the following characteristics, some of them being more important to long-term ecological sustainability than others. These characteristics are expressed in diverse ways; indeed, this diversity of expression is one of the distinctive features of local knowledge.

### Transgenerational Communication That Respects Elder Knowledge

Human communities are best understood as a network of implicit relationships rather than as an aggregate of individuals. Responsible membership in these communities requires understanding which relationships promote the general welfare of both the human and the biotic communities. The relationships are complex, continually changing in response to outside forces, and in constant need of renewal in order to foster the development of community members. As relationships are at the center of community life, they require a more complex form of moral judgment than is usually expressed by individuals who rely on their own limited range of experiences. Local knowledge about relationships that are fair and equitable, as well as ecologically sound, is grounded in the long-term experience of the community. This is not the case when a single generation of individuals engages in a quest to produce new values and technologies for governing relationships. Put another way, local knowledge about relationships, including the relationship of the present generation to future generations, needs to be based on transgenerational communication, where elders keep the larger interests of the community in focus and carry forward the accumulated stock of moral insight about the essentials of long-term relationships.

The elders' role is not to tell the younger generation "how things have always been done in the past," nor is it to pass on the modern myths about how to get ahead at the expense of the group or environment. As the following example of elder knowledge demonstrates, it does not involve imposing divisive biases and often veiled expressions of self-interest upon the younger generation—which is the form of local knowledge that we are most accustomed to in the media and classroom. The following statement by the elders of the Six Nations of the Iroquois Confederation possesses the essential qualities of local knowledge that can be described as intergenerational wisdom:

> Brothers and Sisters: We point out to you the Spiritual Path of Righteousness and Reason. We bring to your thought and minds that right-minded human beings seek to promote above all else the life of all things. We direct to your minds that peace is not merely the absence of war, but the constant effort to maintain harmonious existence between all peoples, from individual to individual and between humans and other beings of this planet. We point out to you that a Spiritual Consciousness is the Path of Survival of Humankind. We who walk about on Mother Earth occupy this place for only a short time. It is our duty as human beings to preserve the life that is here for the benefit of the generations unborn. (Quoted in Moody, 1988, p. 77)

The elders carry forward a cultural intelligence developed over countless generations of communal experience, with its myriad life-affirming relationships. It is profoundly different from the abstract and supposedly objective data that in our culture provides the basis of individual decision making. Furthermore, it is a cultural form of intelligence that provides the conceptual and moral framework for interpreting and acting on the decontextualized data, models, and information acquired through a computer.

Much more deserves to be said about the nature of elder knowledge in order to reverse the misunderstandings of modern thinkers, particularly our tendency to view elders as authoritarian and out of touch with the emerging world of cyberspace. In *Look to the Moun-*

*tain: An Ecology of Indigenous Education* (1994), Gregory Cajete explains the power of the oral tradition carried on by elders:

> The techniques of oral poetry (developed in indigenous societies over countless generations) are designed to *discourage* critical reflection on the stories and their contents, and instead "enchant" the hearers and draw them into the story. This process of enthralling the audience, of impressing upon them the reality of the story, is a central feature of education in oral cultures. Their social institutions are sustained in large part by sound, by what the spoken or sung word can do to commit individuals to particular beliefs, expectations, roles, and behaviors. Thus the techniques of fixing crucial patterns of belief in memory, rhythm, formula, story, and so on, are vitally important. (P. 129, italics added)

As this account of an oral form of cultural renewal suggests, the ideology that computers reinforce is radically different from the ideology that underlies oral traditions of sharing multidimensional forms of local knowledge.

In *Resurgence of the Real: Body, Nature, and Place in a Hypermodern World* (1997), Charlene Spretnak deepens her critique of modernity with a particularly lucid account of earlier critics who have been marginalized and labeled as romantics. Her examination of how critics of industrial modernity, such as Samuel Coleridge, John Ruskin, and William Morris, understood the social pathologies of mechanization and commercialism brings out another aspect of intergenerational knowledge. Their ideas led to the Arts and Crafts Movement, which represented a return to the aesthetic judgment and skill of the worker and to the use of local materials. Although the inspiration came from the religious ideas of Ann Lee rather than the thinkers just mentioned, the Shakers of New England and the Midwest also demonstrated how the design and skill that goes into making a chair or other household objects can combine utility, beauty, and durability and strengthen communal bonds. This approach to work emphasizes mentoring, another aspect of local knowledge that continues to be devalued and disrupted by the characteristics of computers. Mentoring is the practice of passing on to the next generation skills that have their roots in local knowledge. It occurs in most areas of community life: using medicinal plants for healing, performing music, rearing children, playing sports, and various other expressions of craft knowledge. It is profoundly different from the expert forms of knowledge learned in schools, from books, and through computers.

Expert knowledge, in the modern sense, involves knowledge based on theory and experimentation accumulated from sources outside the community. It usually does not take account of local customs and forms of self-sufficiency. The primary distinction, however, between mentoring and the expert knowledge learned through print-based technologies is that mentoring cultivates character, which is one of the results of doing something well. Character includes developing aesthetic judgment, appreciating the integrity of the work at hand, valuing one's service to others, and cultivating the determination and patience to complete a task in a way that meets the high standards set by earlier mentors. Mentoring foregrounds the communal nature of a skill, craft, or performance, rather than the commodified nature of skills increasingly found in education, medicine, law, sports, entertainment, child rearing, and so forth. It places more emphasis on personal skill and character than it does on self-interest and material success.

Within the individualism reinforced in cyberspace, we do not find the qualities of character formation that are at the core of the mentor relationship. Computer-mediated communication can provide access to useful information, model technical procedures, and solve complex problems in highly efficient ways; but it cannot substitute for what is learned through mentoring. While mentoring is important to the survival of local knowledge and interdependency, computers cultivate a personal temperament that is inimitable in a mentoring relationship.

## Knowledge of Place

In *The Practice of the Wild* (1990) Gary Snyder writes that all the inhabitants of place are watching us, whether we are aware of it or not:

> [W]e cannot walk through a meadow or forest without a ripple of report spreading out from one's passage. The thrush darts back, the jay squalls, a beetle scuttles under the grasses, and the signal is passed along. Every creature knows when a hawk is cruising or a human strolling. The information passed through the system is intelligence. (P. 19)

When we take account of the other dimensions of place—water flowing through a stream, grasses, soil, trees, changes in weather—the observant individual will recognize the different forms of information circulating through these life and energy systems. In this context, local knowledge of an environment is especially important for adjusting human behaviors—siting a house, sewing crops, and preserving plant and animal diversity—to ensure minimal environmental impact.

Knowledge of place, when it is deeply embedded in personal experience and understood as an intergenerational responsibility, also includes knowing who were the earlier inhabitants, their technology and economy, and the mythopoetic narratives at the base of their moral community. It also involves knowledge of immediate ancestors and what they learned or failed to learn as they built their community on the moral and conceptual baggage they brought with them in their immigration. We receive this knowledge through stories of their previous experiences with the land. These stories are important aspects of a community of memory that strengthens the sense of connectedness to the welfare of others, including the local biota. The stories also contribute, as Alasdair MacIntyre (1984) reminds us, to a sense of self-identity that reflects the communal relationships experienced over generations. The nomenclature of Western Apache places, as mentioned earlier, illustrates the role that stories play as cultural storehouses of moral insight and human folly. Such a form of cultural coding and storage is far more concentrated than Western approaches to naming the land.

Local knowledge of relationships within the human and biotic communities is learned largely implicitly and contextually, through participatory face-to-face relationships. The anthropologist Edward Hall referred to this as "high-context knowledge" in order to distinguish it from the "low-context knowledge" learned in academic settings, where highly mobile individuals presumably need abstract theory and factual information to utilize in whatever local setting they temporarily find themselves in. Low-context knowledge is acquired from books, book-learned professors, and computer-mediated data and information, which represent a more extreme vehicle. Low-context knowledge is not acquired through relationships encountered in communities that codeveloped over time with changes in the land. Even when based on massive amounts of data, low-context knowledge lacks the accountability intrinsic to face-to-face communication.

Wes Jackson, the codirector of the Land Institute in Kansas, astutely observes the contrast between the current devaluing of local knowledge and the modern, high-status forms of knowledge computers help to promote. In *Altars of Unhewn Stone: Science and the Earth* (1987), he writes,

The culture believes that we are in the midst of an information *explosion* because of the status granted the knowledge accumulated through formal scientific methods. In contrast, knowledge accumulated through tradition, daily experience, and stories, mostly in an informal setting, has little status. We have taken this "folk knowledge" for granted, I suspect, for however *complex* it might be, it was not all that *complicated* to internalize. What we acquired second nature was woven in with the rural setting, the daily work, the local values and moral code. It is more a legacy of the dead than of the living. The more respected body of knowledge, learned through formal discovery or revelation of discovery in classrooms and textbooks, is of a different order. More discipline is involved both in the discovery and in learning about the discovery. And though most of this information is not all that complex, it is more complicated for us to learn and internalize. Maybe this is the reason we assign greater value to such knowledge than to that which we picked up through tradition. There has been an explosion of formal knowledge, but what was necessary to make it accumulate so fast led to the destruction of much of the other older, less formal knowledge. (Pp. 13–14)

It is difficult to discuss the characteristics of local knowledge without highlighting its contributions to viable community relationships and ecological wisdom. Because the prejudice against local (low-status) knowledge runs so deep among the Western-educated elite, I will identify here three areas in which local knowledge is an alternative to ecologically destructive modern trends. First, local knowledge of how to participate in community traditions represents an alternative to the work and consumerism that characterize modern life. For many, consumerism has become an addiction, and for the majority it has become a necessity achieved at the expense of non-commodified relationships and knowledge. While ever-increasing consumerism translates into greater personal debt (now at an all-time high), greater consumption of nonrenewable resources, and greater propagation of toxic wastes, it does not translate into greater employment.

Second, local knowledge is essential to the ecologically appropriate design of technologies and other systems. In the book *Ecological Design* (1996), Sim Van Der Ryn and Stuart Cowan identify five principles that represent a radical shift from an industrial to an ecological approach to design: (1) solutions grow from a knowledge of place; (2) ecological accounting informs the design process; (3) design with nature—work with local natural systems and materials; (4) everyone is a designer—consider the values and traditions of local community; and (5) make nature visible—the design should amplify the natural patterns that have influenced the lives of the people (pp. 54–56).

Third, evidence is beginning to appear in scholarly journals and books that local knowledge of how to mimic nature is the basis of the genetic diversity in the agricultural practices of indigenous cultures. The revival of Andean peasant agriculture, as leaders of the movement describe in Frédérique Apffel-Marglin's *The Spirit of Regeneration: Andean Culture Confronting Western Notions of Development* (1998), and the collection of essays in Wolfgang Sachs's *Global Ecology: The New Arena of Political Conflict* (1993), represent recent efforts to document the connection between local knowledge and genetic diversity. Stephen Marglin's essay "Farmers, Seedmen, and Scientists: Systems of Agriculture and Systems of Knowledge" (1996) provides the most insightful discussion of the differences between indigenous scientific-industrial approaches to agriculture. This literature challenges the myth of primitive agriculture by suggesting that modern science has historically overlooked the connections between ethnic and agricultural diversity. Indigenous agricultural knowledge was accumulated over ten thousand years of careful observation, experimentation, and communal ceremonies that integrated humans into the rhythms of the natural world. Until very recently modern scientists, who ushered in the Green Revolution (which is dependent on mechanization and chemicals) and now want to base the future of agriculture on the genetic re-engineering of Nature, have ignored the achievements of indigenous agriculture. The genius of vernacular agricultural knowledge is that it understands the characteristics of natural systems, which Jackson (1987) describes as the ability to sponsor their own fertility, recycle their nutrients, avoid epidemics from both insects and pathogens, and not lose soil beyond replacement levels. The varieties of rice in Southeast Asia, maize in the American Southwest, and potatoes along the west coast of South America—to cite just a few examples—have not been duplicated by the approach to agriculture that Western scientists and transnational corporations now promote.

The modern trends in agriculture are particularly alarming, especially in light of the rapid growth in world population and consumerism. First, just as our available groundwater supply is diminishing, we are increasingly relying on water-intensive mechanized approaches to agriculture. Second, we have pollution resulting from the pesticides and fertilizers required to produce the crop yields necessary to support capital-intensive agriculture. Third, the growing reliance on transnational corporations that control the new varieties of genetically altered seeds, as well as provide the chemicals and machinery necessary for modern agriculture, is narrowing genetic diversity and contributing to the foreclosure of small farms. In this country the small farmer who often possesses generations of local knowledge is being replaced by university-trained managers and immigrant workers who do not live on the land they farm. The loss of genetic diversity and mixed cropping that characterizes agriculture in many Third World countries is also contributing to destabilizing traditional cultures where agriculture plays an integral role in communal and ceremonial life.

In assessing what is lost as more aspects of cultural life fall sway to computers, the following summary of local knowledge needs to be kept clearly in mind: (1) knowledge of place is cumulative and thus intergenerational—enriched by elder knowledge and communal experiences renewed through stories, ceremonies, and mentoring; (2) local knowledge of ecosystems provides the basis for integrating work and technological practices in ways that cultivate individual skill and moral insight, as well as provide for food and other necessities of community life; (3) the combined knowledge of natural systems and cultural traditions helps ensure that the design of technologies and other material aspects of life serve the continuity of the community rather than undermine it. To reiterate a basic point: this form of knowledge is contextualized, embedded in a community of memory and enhanced through mentoring relationships—all aspects of face-to-face communication that cannot be digitized and computerized without being fundamentally distorted.

## Computer-Reinforced Misconceptions About Data and Information

The arguments that computers "democratize information" and other claims about technological empowerment must be assessed in terms of the accelerating global trends of recent decades: the rapid decline in the viability of natural systems, economic and technological globalization, and the debilitation of alternative cultural traditions. Keeping these trends in mind, I examine the ways in which data and information are both more and less than they seem.

In the following paragraphs I examine whether computers are part of the solution or part of the problem. While we have yet to learn how Bill Gates, Sherry Turkle, and the other computer futurists would explain the impact of computer-driven technologies, I want to suggest that computers and their subsequent subculture are accelerating the more destructive aspects of the trends just mentioned. This judgment takes full account of the many ways in which computers help solve complex technical problems and facilitate communication. Before computers, we—except for managers who were attempting to fit work routines to the principles of scientific efficiencies promised by Taylorism—performed our tasks, whether solving technical problems or communicating by phone or mail, without being overly concerned about efficiency. Perhaps we had a simpler understanding of our problems. The pace of life was slower and less dependent upon data, but I cannot recall any situation (except in the theoretical sciences) where critical decisions could not be made because of technological limitations.

The global trends mentioned earlier seem to be of a radically different order of importance. Changes in the chemical and genetic makeup of life systems, the replacement of craft knowledge with computer-driven machines, and emergence of electronic communities (with the accompanying loss of local knowledge) involve fundamentally different consequences for humankind than our precomputer dilemmas, which resulted from the technological inability to communicate data instantaneously or to collect data on people's behavior.

As Gregory Bateson (1972) puts it, "the computer is only an arc of a larger circuit, which always includes a man and an environment, from which information is received and upon which different messages from the computers have effect" (p. 317). As part of a larger cultural ecology, data and information encode and reproduce the deepest assumptions underlying the cultural group's way of knowing, even as they appear to be bias-free representations of the real world. Partly to maintain the semblance of political neutrality and partly to uphold the seemingly culture-free quality of rational thinking, modern thinkers maintain that observation that adheres to modern research protocols yield objective data. Like a camera, observation provides an accurate account of real-life phenomena. Measurements by instruments, according to this way of thinking, yield data and information that are even more free of subjective interpretation and cultural bias. This naive view, which universities and their university-educated experts ardently embrace, has been under attack for years by philosophers of science such as Paul Feyerabend (1975) and Sandra Harding (1988). That it continues to be promoted within the computer subculture leads to one of the major ironies in the global promotion of computers as a technology of personal empowerment. Web sites, such as that of the Library of Congress, contain a wealth of information compiled over generations of scholarly effort. Other web sites have the same appearance of objectivity but may have been produced by anonymous individuals who may be as unaware of their own cultural biases as the people who visit the web site. As all symbolic representations reproduce the assumptions of their cultural group, even the information obtained by visiting scholarly web sites is less than it seems. It lacks the objectivity it is assumed to possess.

Data and information lack authority (except for those who have been socialized to certain conventions of thought) because their authorship, along with their cultural and historical contexts, are lost in print-based encoding and communicating. The technology that allows a search engine to locate thousands of references to a particular word or topic, while creating the impression that the collected knowledge of humankind is instantly accessible anywhere in the world, cannot reproduce what we most need to know in order to make judgments about the context that the data and information are extracted from. Without a knowledge of the context and an ability to enter into the consciousness of the cultural group that the data and information purport to represent, computer use adds another layer of interpretation to the previously existing interpretive layers that have been passed along, sometimes over generations, as objective.

Everything that appears on a computer screen is given technological equality. The data and information in a hate group's web site, or the fictitious data an individual with an alias persona exchanges with other participants in a chat room, appear as objectively as the data on the web site of the Smithsonian Institution. With everything appearing as equally objective, discrimination is left to individual judgment. The reduction of any life experience and insight to the superficial forms of knowledge that we call data and information requires the judgment of individuals who are far removed from the originating contexts to make any real assessment of veracity. Most computer advocates and educators agree with this use of individual judgment and regard it as empowerment, and further argue that this is why computers are a technological breakthrough in human learning. Unfortunately, this form of individualism has proven highly susceptible to manipulation by forces promoting consumerism and is indifferent to intergenerational and environmental responsibility. A combination of educational forces—the increasing emphasis on data as the basis of thinking, more reliance on computers in the classroom, and the abdication of the teacher's responsibility suggested in the slogan that they should be as "a guide on the side"— leaves an increasing number of individuals without the contextual knowledge and theoretical perspectives necessary for recognizing the limitations of data and information. For them, what appears on the screen will seem true, and they will interpret it in terms of a cultural schema they are unaware of.

Computer-mediated data and information strengthens the modern belief that objectivity and fact are separate from values. As I argued earlier, facts and information are communicated in the symbolic language of a particular cultural group. Since language is used to communicate about relationships, there is always a question of how to act in these relationships. Relationships are thus a matter of moral judgment. Generally, the moral codes built up over generations of cultural experience are encoded and reproduced in the language.

To recognize that language reproduces the moral templates of the cultural group raises the question, What is the morality hidden by the modern myth that data are separate from values? The prevailing misconception about the separation between data and values does not seem to prevent individuals from using data as the basis for making decisions about relationships. Too often the supposed objectivity of the data has been used to justify the seemingly rational nature of the decision. This discussion may appear to be about issues that have little relevance to the more visible problems of disintegrating communities and the headlong rush to economically exploit the environment. When we compare the "data" about the environment that are intergenerationally communicated in more ecologically centered cultures with the seemingly objective data on the computer screen, we can see that the moral orientation inherent in the latter cultural approach is profoundly different. In this difference we find that the modern view of data and information is not only less than what it seems, but totally inadequate as a way of understanding our moral relationship to the environment.

In traditional, ecologically centered cultures, information about plants, animals, and other aspects of the environment is framed to foreground the moral nature of the relationship between humans and the environment. It is not presented as an objective matter of personal decision making; rather, the knowledge is learned along with the cultural group's codes of moral reciprocity. In contrast, computer-mediated data and information reinforces the anthropocentric and instrumental moral orientation that have been the hallmark of the Industrial Revolution. While helping to maintain the myth that high-status knowledge is not compromised by self-serving political interests, these reductionist forms of knowledge are inadequate to rectify the problem of moral blindness. While computers may increase our ability to engage in instrumental relationships, they should be understood as contributing to the loss of moral and spiritual knowledge about how to live sustainably within our environment.

The previous discussion focused on the cultural amnesia that accompanies the elevated status of data- and information-dominated culture. The larger circuit (or larger ecology) that computers are part of, to recall Bateson's observation, includes the growing influence of experts whose authority is legitimized by their ability to locate data to support their latest recommendations. Experts now influence behavior, thought, and values in nearly every area of materialist community life: how we should vote, what we should eat, how we manipulate individual vulnerabilities to market products. Indeed, current changes introduced into modern culture are conceptualized, directed, and continually evaluated by experts who rely on computers to assess how best to influence public behavior. The role of experts in modern society was well established before the appearance of computers, but computers have expanded their number and given further legitimacy to their continual quest to provide expert guidance.

One of the most important characteristics of modern experts is their aggressive efforts to commodify activities, forms of knowledge, and social relationships that previously were the basis of reciprocal responsibility and bonding in communities. The search is for the niche market—whether in interpersonal communication, education, leisure activity, mentoring, or biotechnology. This connection between expert forms of knowledge and the commodification of the community does not mean that all forms of expert knowledge are destructive or that they are always motivated by a desire for economic gain. This is far from the case. But the modern expert, regardless of whether she or he makes a beneficial contribution or fosters still more consumerism, undermines the essential characteristics of local knowledge. These include intergenerational communication (including elder knowledge), knowledge of place, engagement in noncommodified relationships and activities that support the community, and thinking and communicating in the vernacular that enforces the moral codes for guiding human-to-nature relationships. The modern expert, now armed with computers, is educated in the high-status patterns of thinking learned in the university. Of the many detrimental characteristics of high-status knowledge, one of the most destructive is the emphasis on diagnosing problems and framing solutions as models that can be replicated in various cultural contexts. Another is the assumption that abstract, theoretical, and data-based knowledge is more enlightened, progressive, and effective than knowledge learned and tested over generations of cultural experience within an ecological context. The latter has long been recognized by marginalized cultural groups as one of the reasons for the failure of expert forms of knowledge, but their insights have been ignored because of the supposed backwardness of their cultures. Even if the experts possessed sufficient knowledge of other cultures to write software programs that would allow for the simulation of superficial cultural patterns, their communication through the computer would send a powerful cultural message: the computer and the mind-set that created it are more advanced than the cultural group whose local knowledge has been catalogued and digitized.

The statement that data and information are more than they seem takes on additional significance when we consider the connections between computer-mediated thought and communication and the secularization that has been part of modernization. The relationships between modern technology (particularly computers), secularization, and the ecological crisis are very complex. Because the clarification of these relationships necessitates questioning the moral (indeed, sacred) foundations of modern beliefs and institutions, they will be addressed in the next chapter—but within the context of the scientific metanarrative that is often interpreted to justify the "survival of the fittest."

# 4 Evolutionary Theory and the Global Computer Culture

When the North American Free Trade Agreement with Mexico (NAFTA) went into effect in January 1994, thousands of Indians in Chiapas rebelled against this latest expression of modern economic development. Their struggle to retain their traditions in the face of international trade agreements led them to armed insurrection against the local representatives of the Mexican government; it also led them to use the Internet to communicate their demands to the outside world. Computer technology enabled them to communicate with international groups that eventually brought pressure on the Mexican government to switch from using tanks, fighter aircraft, and helicopters against the rebels and begin negotiations with them.

On a trip in 1998 to the village of Guelatao high in the Sierra de Juárez Mountains of Mexico, I met with three young men who had come to the birthplace of Benito Juárez (the George Washington of the Mexican Revolution) to help the assembly of village elders communicate their ancestral knowledge to the young people, who are becoming increasingly influenced by modern media and their corresponding values. Through videos, radio programs, and the Internet, the young men were attempting to educate the local youth to recognize the importance of traditional forms of knowledge to solve environmental and community problems and to remain independent of outside experts who exacerbated their impoverishment and the loss of cultural identity. The Internet was seen as especially important for communicating with other indigenous cultures around the world facing similar challenges.

There are many other examples of such efforts to use computers to preserve cultural traditions against the eroding pressures of modernization. Indeed, numerous others could easily be cited, including using computers to preserve languages on the verge of extinction. This use of the technology is generally justified on the grounds that the technology is neutral. Whether it has a constructive or destructive impact, so the argument goes, depends on the intent of its users. The young men in Guelatao expressed this view, and I have heard it expressed by audiences in several European cities where I gave talks on the cultural bias inherent in computers. The audience's questions—"Weren't people also concerned about the introduction of the railroad?"—were raised as though questioning the cultural impact of computers would prove to be as pointless as questioning the wisdom of this earlier technology.

Not only indigenous cultures use computers to preserve traditional forms of knowledge and moral authority. Religious groups, particularly in North America, have used the Internet to transform themselves into a powerful political force that now influences the national debate on myriad educational and moral issues and government policies. Their ability to sustain themselves on the national level as an electronic interest group further threatens to undermine the separation of church and state that has been an ideal (though not always a practice) of liberal democracy.

The widely held perception that computer technology is either neutral or brings more benefits than losses ignores a fundamental aspect of the cultural baggage that accompanies their use. In addition to the patterns of thinking described in earlier chapters (the subjectivity of cyberspace and the differences between data and local knowledge), the arguments for globalizing computers reinforce an increasingly powerful and often ignored metanarrative. Scientists who are attempting to explain the fundamental processes that continue to shape life on this planet are still constructing this metanarrative, which is commonly known as the evolution of the species. While recent developments in molecular and evolutionary biology further strengthen this metanarrative, it has problematic implications that should be addressed in any discussion of the cultural effects of computer technology. This chapter will examine the connections between computers and the issues that surround the use of the metanarrative to justify what is euphemistically called "convergent cultural change." Special attention will be given to how computer proponents frame advances in computer technology as part of evolution. Understanding how evolution theory is used to portray computers as both a form of cultural progress, and a postbiological stage of evolution clarifies why computer proponents ignore differences in cultural ways of knowing and the culturally based moral values that govern human-to-nature relationships.

Disturbingly, influential computer proponents invoke evolution theory to explain why some cultures have "evolved" further than others, citing the "fitness" of organisms to survive in their environment and the competition between organisms to ensure their own reproductive success. As the analysis of the writings of the more prominent computer proponents will show, these elements of evolution theory are also used to explain why cultures that retain their noncommodified and non-computer-mediated traditions will disappear as naturally as other poorly adapted species. In effect, the theory of evolution is being used to turn the slogan "survival of the fittest" (which has become a moral code in the computer industry) into a moral principle for guiding relationships between cultures. Evolutionary theory, as interpreted by such writers as Moravec (1988), Kelly (1994), and Stock (1993), also serves the economic interests of the small yet powerful group of symbolic engineers who are working to make the indigenous cultures, such as the village of Guelatao, into digitally preserved artifacts to be stored in a CD-ROM.

Embedding our understanding of computers in an evolutionary framework creates a serious double bind: the theory of evolution, for all its power to explain biology, is unsuitable for explaining the impact of computers on the world's diverse cultural ways of knowing. Among the confusion that arises when this separation is not maintained is the tendency to equate Western technological progress with the design process of Nature. This tendency is especially prevalent in the writings of computer proponents identified in the following analysis.

## Evolution Theory and Our Current Thinking About Computers

The early days of Artificial Intelligence research and theorizing were characterized by the claim that, in a few years, computers would outperform human intelligence. The 1999 announcement that MIT's Big Blue beat the current world chess champion, Garry Kasparov, represented a muted celebration of another step in the evolutionary process. The professional and popular literature that explains the uses and future prospects of computers interprets change as an inevitable process of Nature. The implicit interpretation of computers as an expression of evolution is clearly present in the writings of Turkle (1996a, 1996b), Negroponte (1995), and other computer advocates. Turkle continually refers to how computers are facilitating the transition from a modern to a postmodern culture of "opacity, playful experimentation, and navigation of surface as privileged ways of knowing" (1996a, p. 267). Her way of understanding the linear direction of cultural changes fuses Western-style progress with natural evolution, making the latter less discernible. That computers should be interpreted as a natural and inevitable part of human evolution is also an assumption that underlies Negroponte's prediction that

[E]arly in the next millennium your right and left cufflinks or earrings may communicate with each other by low-orbiting satellites

and have more computer power than your present PC. Your telephone won't ring indiscriminately; it will receive, sort, and perhaps
respond to your incoming calls like a well-trained English butler.
Mass media will be redefined by systems of transmitting and receiving personalized information and entertainment. Schools will
change to become more like museums and playgrounds for children to assemble ideas and socialize with other children all over the
world. The digital planet will look and feel like the head of a pin.
(1995, p. 5)

Steven R. Holtzman (1994) envisions computer-human evolution on an even more convergent pathway:

[T]he software of the future will be programs that run on your computer: your mind. Games will be entertaining experiences: worlds
that you play in. A database of information will be in the form that
allows you to access it while thinking, directly enhancing your memory. And books, music, and films will become the recording of the
neural sensations to think an idea, experience the soul vibrating with
sound, and participate in a virtual reality. Rather than reading, listening, or viewing, a recording will directly evoke the experience of
what we feel and what we emote. (P. 209)

Both Negroponte and Holtzman interpret the evolutionary process as leading to a consumer utopia of immediate individual grati-
fication. Alan C. Kay (1991), writing about the educational uses
of computers, engages in the more common practice of combining
the evolutionary paradigm with Western ethnocentrism when he
claims that computer literacy will enable students to escape the "bar-
barism of the deep past" and "learn new paradigms for viewing the
world" (p. 140). Kay's statement reflects an assumption shared by
others who rely on the interpretive framework of human (and, by
extension, cultural) evolution: that preliterate cultures were primitive and barbaric, while contemporary literate cultures are complex
and progressive.

The writings of George Bugliarello (1990), Hans Moravec (1988), Gregory Stock (1993), and Kevin Kelly (1994) further illustrate the explicit interpretation of computers as a vehicle of evolution. As their thinking raises fundamental questions that I will examine later, it would be best if the connections were stated in their own words. For example, Bugliarello explains the evolutionary process leading to what he terms *hyperintelligence* in the following way:

> When we first emerged from the trees as hominids, our intelligence was primarily biological and only to a very limited extent social. . . . Our biological intelligence has remained basically unchanged for at least the past 50,000 years. However, in the last forty years, in combination with social intelligence, it has begun to give birth to computers and what can be called "machine intelligence". . . . We are now at the point in which the global networks I have described, the progressions from the brain with its billions of neurons, to the node, as I have defined it, begin to constitute a global brain. This is constituted of nodes—each a human brain with some $10^{11}$ neurons plus a computer with some $10^6$ memory elements, linked via the socio-machine interconnections to $10^7$ other nodes, all made technically possible in real time by fiber optics. In this global brain each element of a node—human brain, computer, and interconnections—begins to have comparable capacity, if not yet comparable complexity. We can thus begin to talk of a hyperbrain. . . . The hyperbrain and hyperintelligence may be viewed as a new step in the evolutionary development of the species. (1990, pp. 28–29)

The statements by Moravec, Stock, and Kelly quoted in an earlier chapter also represent change as an expression of natural selection. Indeed, we can see in their writings the evolutionary paradigm in its most rigid, reductionist, and deterministic form. Moravec's announcement that computers signal the transition to the "postbiological" phase of evolution makes any discussion of alternative expressions of cultural development appear as entirely pointless. In the chapter headings and subheadings of Stock's book *Metaman* (1993), one can see the misinterpretation of evolution as linear: "Organisms and Superorganisms," "Crossing the Threshold," "Toward Machine Intelligence," "In Biology's Footsteps," "An Evolving Global Brain," "Toward Global Culture," "Biological Design Comes of Age," and "The Evolution of Evolution."

As the following quote illustrates, Stock's interpretation of the emerging computerized intelligence contains the key elements of the evolutionary paradigm that are so problematic when used to explain the development of cultures:

> Metaman, like a *developing* organism, manifests change within itself rather than in its progeny, but Metaman changes by unprogrammed adaptation that is decidedly *evolutionary* in character. Indeed, just as biological evolution rests on changes in genetic information, progressive change within Metaman also rests upon modifications in information, advances in scientific knowledge, technology, institutional structures, laws, economic systems. (1993, p. 227)

A dominant theme in Kevin Kelly's book *Out of Control* (1994) is also an important part of Stock's argument about the inevitability of evolving beyond our present-day individual and cultural expression. As Stock, who holds a Ph.D. in biophysics from Johns Hopkins University, puts it, the evolution of Metaman "requires no coherent plan; it simply happens" (p. 187).

In effect, the transition to the postbiological phase of evolution, referred to loosely as cyberspace and the Information Age, is, according to Kelly, out of our control. The organizing principles that drive both biological evolution and computer and software design will lead to the convergence that Kelly calls a neobiological civilization: a "world of mutating buildings, living silicon polymers, software programs evolving off-line, adaptable cars, rooms stuffed with co-evolutionary furniture, gnatbots for learning, manufactured biological viruses that cure your illnesses, neural jacks, cyborian body parts, designer food crops, simulated personalities, and a vast ecology of computing devices in constant flux" (1994, p. 472). To quote again a key part of Kelly's argument, nothing, including the development of computer technology, escapes the logic of evolution:

> We should not be surprised that life, having subjugated the bulk of inert matter on Earth, would go on to subjugate technology, and bring it also under its reign of constant evolution, perpetual novelty, and an agenda out of our control. Even without the control we must surrender, a neo-biological technology is far more rewarding than a world of clocks, gears, and predictable simplicity. (P. 472)

Kelly does not mention that natural selection (which is indeed out of our control) has no predetermined direction. He nevertheless incorporates into his futuristic vision the Western myth that equates evolutionary progress with technological development.

## Natural Evolution As a Cultural Metanarrative

There is an interesting parallel between the arguments of Stock and Kelly and the views of scientists who believe that the scientific method is the only valid approach to knowledge. The two positions are mutually reinforcing, and both deny the legitimacy of other cultural ways of knowing and developing—including those based on ecological sustainability. The claim that all aspects of cultural development are subject to the logic of biological evolution (which now includes technological evolution) leaves no basis for resisting what is in reality the digital phase of the Industrial Revolution. To claim that cultural developments are out of our control is no different from the Biblical examples of creating objects and then projecting onto them absolute power over their creators. (One such example of this is the effort of a researcher at Stanford University's Center for the Study of

Language and Information to develop the technology that utilizes the brain's electrical activity as the basis of interacting with computers.) There is a difference, however, in locating absolute control in a metanarrative that has its origins in modern scientific epistemology. Stock's and Kelly's arguments abdicate moral responsibility for the destructive impact of computers by claiming that cultural developments that meet Nature's long-term test of survival and replication represent the logic of Nature.

In the book published the year he died, *The Demon-Haunted World* (1997), Carl Sagan explains the efficacy of the scientist's approach to knowledge:

> [T]he reason science works so well is partly that built-in error-correcting machinery. There are no forbidden questions in science, no matters too sensitive or delicate to be probed, no sacred truths. That openness to new ideas, combined with the most rigorous, skeptical scrutiny of all ideas, sifts the wheat from the chaff. It makes no difference how smart, august or beloved you are. Diversity and debate are valued. Opinions are encouraged to contend—substantively and in depth. . . . We insist on independent and—to the extent possible—quantitative verification of proposed tenets of belief. We are constantly prodding, challenging, seeking contradictions or small, persistent residual errors, proposing alternative explanations, encouraging heresy. We give our highest rewards to those who convincingly disprove established beliefs. (Pp. 34–35)

The testing of ideas and conventional wisdom, a hypothesis against empirical evidence in experimental settings, and a need for other scientists to meet the test of replication point to the principal cultural characteristic of scientific epistemology: the expectation that changes resulting from scientific inquiry (including technologies based on scientific discoveries) will contribute to human progress. The reverse side of the coin is that ways of knowing, forms of moral authority, and traditions grounded in nonscientific forms of authority are expressions of ignorance, superstition, and quackery—or, as Sagan puts it, the darkness of a demon-haunted world.

The arguments of computer proponents that Nature's logic makes Western technological development and consumerism inevitable and irresistible, and Sagan's argument that scientific inquiry is the only valid way of advancing knowledge, lead to a serious double bind in addressing the ecological crisis. In spite of the strengths Sagan identifies, science cannot provide the basis of moral values that should govern relationships within the cultural and natural commons. Nor can it provide the moral justification for cultures that are resisting the forces of modernization—particularly since science has provided the basic knowledge for developing the technologies upon which modernity is based. However, the metanarrative that represents all forms of life and, by extension, the technologies of cultures as evolving carries moral implications.

While most scientists disclaim responsibility for the political and economic uses of their discoveries, as well as reject the criticism that they benefit the interests of a particular cultural (now transcultural) group, they nevertheless engage in a cultural experiment with the symbolic foundations of cultures that, in turn, places more pressure on the life-sustaining capacities of natural systems. The thousands of synthetic chemicals introduced into the environment over the last half-century are just one aspect of this cultural experiment. Advances in computer technology, which depend on scientific research, are yet another aspect of the cultural experiment, which is now going global. The dominant metanarrative to justify these experiments as a continuation of evolution provides an important reason for critically examining the current uses of science as a source of legitimation.

The following discussion should not be interpreted as an attack on the scientific method or as a lack of appreciation for the cultural benefits of scientific discoveries. It should be interpreted as questioning the myth that scientific discoveries and modes of inquiry do not reflect the political, economic, and epistemological orientation of a cultural group. It should also be interpreted as questioning the hubris that underlies a long tradition of scientific support for cultural approaches to development that have proven to be ecologically destructive—starting with the Industrial Revolution and continuing today with the spread of Western-style individualism and consumerism through computer technology. More specifically, this analysis should raise basic questions about the influence of a metanarrative that makes competition and the "selfish gene" the basis for explaining why certain individual and cultural traits survive while others do not. When the surviving individual and cultural traits contribute to the loss of noncommodified community and environmental relationships, we must ask whether the cultural uses of science now contribute to our ecological crisis and our loss of cultural diversity.

The metanarrative, which was first fully elaborated in Darwin's *On the Origin of Species* (1859), is the story of how different organisms, including humans, evolved by adapting to environmental changes. It's a familiar narrative learned in most public school science classes: the evolution of humans, as we know ourselves today, began over four million years ago with primitive hominids wandering the savannas and woodlands of Africa. While Darwin's theory of evolution explained the role Nature (specifically, climate, food, and enemies) plays in selecting which traits will survive in later generations and in the evolution of species, in recent years the narrative has been modified to take account of how changes in DNA alter the chemistry of proteins that, in turn, give rise to new traits in the organism.

The modern synthesis that characterizes today's version of natural selection is based on the research findings of population genetics, evolutionary biology, cell biology, and molecular biology. This synthesis holds that spontaneous mutations in DNA produce new traits in the organism, which make it either more or less likely to survive and reproduce. Among a whole population, the offspring of the genetically "fittest" individuals will thus, over several generations, come to dominate. As this summary does not adequately foreground the determining role that genes play in the development of cells that lead to organism, behavior, and thus culture, it is important to consider E. O. Wilson's more elegantly nuanced explanation (1998):

> The genes prescribing the epigenetic rules of the brain and behavior are only segments of giant molecules. *They feel nothing, care for nothing, intend nothing.* Their role is to trigger the sequences of chemical reactions within the highly structured fertilized cell that orchestrate epigenesis. Their writ extends to the levels of molecule, cell, and organ. This early state of epigenesis, consisting of a series of sequential physiochemical reactions, culminates in the self-assembly of the sensory system and brain. Only then, when the organism is completed, does mental activity appear as an emergent process. (P. 165, italics added)

Wilson goes on to qualify the genetic determinism in this explanation by saying that "across evolutionary time, the aggregate of choices of many brains determine the Darwinian fate of everything human—the genes, the epigenetic rules, the communicating minds, and the culture." It is critically important to note that his effort to give culture a coevolutionary role is not based on scientific research but on extrapolations from animal behavior and from arguments buttressed by highly selective evidence of macrocultural trends.

At first glance, Wilson's account of nonfeeling, noncaring, nonintending genes self-replicating (with occasional internal and external glitches) supports the thesis of Stock and Kelly that the operation of Nature is out of our control. Recent technical applications of this growing body of knowledge, however, represent a major economic growth industry built on the assumption that scientists know how to design improved forms of life. Genetic engineering thus represents a radical form of human intervention in the survival-of-the-fittest logic of Nature. Computers have been essential to establishing the knowledge base for this synthesis and to providing the technology for subsequent interventions in genetic coding.

However, it is the extension of natural selection theory to purportedly account for the development of culture (including values, behaviors, and institutions) that is most relevant to understanding the problem of regarding computers as evolutionary. This extension, which carries the same name as E. O. Wilson's *Sociobiology: The New Synthesis* (1975), argues that human capacities and cultural forms of expression are biologically determined. Thus, all aspects of culture, from its symbolic language, aesthetics, and technologies to patterns of cooperation and child rearing, can be traced back to the adaptive traits of individuals, which in turn can be traced back to the information coded in the genes. In *Promethean Fire: Reflections on the Origins of Mind* (1983), Wilson and coauthor Charles J. Lumsden summarize the basic extension that sociobiology makes to the evolutionary metanarrative:

> The main postulate is that certain unique and remarkable properties of the human mind result in a tight linkage between genetic evolution and cultural history. The human genes affect the way that the mind is formed—which stimuli are perceived and which missed, how information is processed, the kinds of memories most easily recalled, the emotions they are most likely to evoke, and so forth. The processes that create such effects are called the epigenetic rules. The rules are rooted in the particularities of human biology, and they influence the way culture is formed. (P. 20)

As these epigenetic rules become encoded in cultural norms and practices, culture, in turn, enables individuals who adhere to these norms and practices to survive and reproduce more successfully. But the origin of culture is in the "selfish gene" that seeks to pass on its hereditary characteristics in an environment where other individuals, including other organisms, are competing to reproduce themselves. Thus, the same process of natural selection at work between organisms is also at work within cultures—as well as between cultures. Success (or progress, to use a more culturally laden term) is a matter of which organism or cultural practice is most biologically adapted and thus most likely to reproduce itself. Wilson reiterates this basic argument in his 1998 book *Consilience: The Unity of Knowledge.*

Richard D. Alexander's *The Biology of Moral Systems* (1987) purports to add another dimension to the explanatory power of sociobiology. Contrary to the arguments that locate moral behavior in individual rational or emotive judgment, socialization to cultural norms, or encoded linguistic and cultural characteristics, Alexander claims that moral behavior is the expression of individual interests. And the most basic interest is to "promote the survival of the individual's genetic material" (p. 37). This interest may lead to moral behaviors such as cooperation, altruism, and even self-sacrifice. According to Alexander, these acts of "individuals producing and aiding offspring and, in some species, aiding other descendents and some nondescendent relatives as well" increase chances of genetic survival. While Alexander argues that "we are evolved to serve the interests of our genes," he also acknowledges that we may choose moral behaviors that are contrary to "increased success in reproduction." But the moral decisions not taken in the interest of genetic survival are contrary to "what their evolutionary background has prepared them to do" (p. 40).

Mary Clark, a retired biology professor now living in Oregon, summarizes the evolutionary metanarrative and foregrounds several key issues that serve as a starting point for examining the connections between evolution theory and the spread of computerization. According to Clark, the widely taught, overly simplified evolutionary paradigm (including that of sociobiology) is based on the following assumptions, which, she argues, are too restrictive:

> [T]hat scarcity and competition shape the biotic world; that the "unit of selection" is the gene or, at most, the individual organism, and that all else is "environment" to which the individual is maximally adapted; that selection pressure has been and is constantly present for all species; . . . that a high level of species diversity generates stability in the ecosystem; and that evolution is "progressive." (P. 25)

### Sociobiology, Computers, and Survival of the Fittest

Moral values supposedly fall outside the domain of scientific inquiry. Nevertheless, the representation of life as genetically driven within a competitive environment to pass on hereditary traits and ensure future survival provides a biologically based moral framework. The sociobiology argument also makes competition the basic relationship between cultures. As its critic R. C. Lewontin (1992) summarizes, "Genes make individuals, and individuals make culture, so genes make culture." This moral framework, which can also be viewed as an ideology that justifies subverting the viability of other cultures, is made explicit in his criticisms of what this metanarrative attempts to explain and justify. In *Biology As Ideology: The Doctrine of DNA* (1992), Lewontin, the holder of the Alexander Agassiz chair in zoology at Harvard University, notes that the sociobiology theory of human nature and its relationship to culture is based on a three-step argument:

> The first is a description of what human nature is like. . . . The second is to claim that those characteristics that appear to be universal

are, in fact, coded in our genes, that is in our *DNA*. There are genes for religiosity, genes for entrepreneurship, genes for whatever characteristics are said to be built into the human psyche and human social organization. The theory thus goes on to the third step, the claim that natural selection, through differential survival and reproduction of different kinds of organisms, has led inevitably to the particular genetic characteristics of human beings, characteristics that are responsible for the form of society. This claim strengthens the argument of legitimacy because it goes beyond mere description to assert that the human nature described is inevitable, given the *universal law of the struggle for existence and the survival of the fittest.* (Pp. 89–90, italics added)

Given Lewontin's observation, one can see the ideological significance of the more explicit paradigm that frames how Morevec, Stock, and Kelly understand the cultural transforming potential of computers. The forms of abstract intelligence, relationships, and communication that computers privilege over face-to-face communities represent for them the next inevitable stage of evolution. Indeed, the symbolic systems that make cyberspace possible express the latest stage of evolution that surpasses the genetic capacities that left individuals (and cultures) stuck at the more primitive level of storing wisdom about relationships in narratives and dance, being dependent upon context as a source of meaning, and relying on experiential knowledge and moral accountability. The "global superorganism" Stock envisions, the computers that Moravec predicts will take over after humans have downloaded their "mental activities" and faded into the evolutionary historical record, and the "bionic hybrids" that Kelly foresees reflect the superior "genetic fitness" of their creators. To challenge these developments would be futile, as they are, in their view, the result of Nature's evolutionary process.

There is a moral imperative even in the more implicit interpretation of evolution that leads Negroponte and Turkle to see progress in the transition to the limitless freedoms of cyberspace. Individuals whose genetic makeup endows them with a high tolerance for simulated interactions and the nonlinear nature of texts would be acting immorally if they were to deviate from what the history of natural selection has programmed them for. According to scientific theory, evolution has no predetermined future; but as an ideology, it has a distinct cultural trajectory. Like the earlier Social Darwinists who used literacy as one of the gauges for locating different cultures in the evolutionary scale, this new ideology upholds the culture of cyberspace and bionic hybrids as the latest manifestations of Nature that other cultures must emulate—if they are to survive. There is an additional similarity between the futuristic vision of cyberspace advocates and the exemplary models of the earlier Social Darwinists. Both used the technological achievements of Western cultures as evidence of what the future holds for the seemingly less-evolved cultures.

Noticeably absent from the futuristic predictions of computer advocates is an in-depth discussion of the possibility that the losses connected with the transition to cyberspace might overwhelm the gains. In the last pages of her book, Turkle (1996a) suggests the need for caution: "The culture of simulation," she writes, "may help us achieve a vision of a multiple but integrated identity . . . with access to our many selves. But if we have lost reality in the process, we have struck a poor bargain" (p. 268). This warning, which she makes from her perspective as a clinical psychologist who is focused on the need for self-knowledge, seems like a superficially formed and totally marginal afterthought to the real issues that most of the world's population now face.

The explicit and more orthodox interpretation of the place of computers in evolution makes it unnecessary for Moravec, Stock, and Kelly to consider whether computers might undermine the symbolic foundations of cultures that have not formed commodified relationships and exploited the environment. Contrary to their thinking, the "fittest" cultures may be the ones that, in defining wealth in terms other than economic and technological progress and access to decontextualized data, have minimized their impact on local ecosystems. One of the ironies in the definition of cultural evolution, in the eyes of both computer futurists and Social Darwinists of the last century, is that these cultures leave a larger environmental footprint than cultures that have been regarded as backward and primitive. To recall the figures cited earlier, the environmental footprint of North Americans requires 5.1 hectares of land to sustain their life-style and to recycle the resulting wastes, while the average environmental footprint in India is 0.4 hectares.

As futurist literature predicts the inevitable merger of cultures into the common culture of cyberspace, I shall identify a number of cultural and ecological issues that should not be ignored in the rush to "evolve" to the next stage of existence.

## *Cultural Diversity and Ecological Sustainability*

The cultural mediating characteristics of computers (discussed in previous chapters) make computers a culture-transforming technology. When computers are introduced into cultures with different root metaphors and mythopoetic narratives, they further reinforce the form of subjectivity, experience of time, human-centeredness, moral relativism, and other characteristics of Western modernity. Many social elites of these cultures learned through their exposure to Western education to assume Western thought patterns and values. Computers help to spread these ideas and values among the larger segments of the local population that have not received Western-style education. In contributing to what Vandana Shiva calls the "monoculture of the mind," computers undermine traditional forms of cultural knowledge and patterns of relationships. Within certain circles of Western thinkers, arguments have been made that this intellectual and economic colonialism is morally wrong.

I would like to think that these arguments are still taken seriously. But exchanges with academic colleagues in various settings have led me to believe that most of them tend to view these arguments as hopelessly romantic. In addition to citing examples of traditional cultures that have retained morally problematic practices, such as female circumcision, critics of cultural pluralism often claim that American Indians were as environmentally destructive as the European immigrants—as if this unsubstantiated claim justifies the line of thinking that upholds Western modernity as morally superior. The modern emphasis on moral subjectivity further undercuts the argument that we should not use our yardstick of economic and technological development as the basis of judging other cultures. When we use Western categories for determining which cultures are developed and which are developing, the moral issues associated with colonialism tend to disappear under the weight of the West's moral certainty that it has a "responsibility" to help these cultures attain the benefits of a Western form of development.

The argument against globalizing our computer-based culture should thus be framed on more pragmatic grounds: namely, it is in everyone's self-interest that the distinctive cultural traditions of knowledge that developed over hundreds, even thousands of years within a bioregion not be lost. It is also in everyone's self-interest that cultural traditions that have proven successful in maintaining the local community's economic and technological self-sufficiency do not disappear as a result of the pressure to become modern, consumer-oriented, data-based thinkers. There is now abundant evidence that traditional, bioregionally oriented cultures developed a complex understanding of how to meet their physical and symbolic needs by learning about their local environment—and framing their understanding, which involved modifying their environment, within a moral framework rooted in their mythopoetic narratives. According to the findings of field biologist Edgar Anderson, who published *Plants, Man, and Life* in 1967, the groundedness of cultural groups in Nature led to the greatest expansion in the genetic basis of edible plants. More recently, other observers—Wes Jackson (1987), Shiv Visvanathan (1997), Gustavo Esteva (1996), Vandana Shiva (1993), and Frédérique Apffel-Marglin and Stephen Marglin (1996), among others—have begun to document the connections between knowledge embedded in intergenerational experience with local plants, animals, soil conditions, weather patterns, and so forth, and sustainable agricultural practices. Commodified farming practices, by contrast—the increasing use of fertilizers, pesticides, and genetic engineering—are the basis of modern agriculture and have narrowed the gene pool that traditional cultures expanded over thousands of years of integrating agricultural and cultural knowledge.

In his careful analysis of the differences between high-tech agriculture and indigenous agricultural knowledge, Stephen A. Marglin (1996) indirectly summarizes the argument for genuine cultural diversity. While Marglin is not addressing the role of computers, his analysis of high-tech agriculture identifies the cultural patterns that computers magnify: decontextualized knowledge and technologies that are universally applied, a disregard (even disdain) for local knowledge and cultural traditions, and a promotion of technologies that benefit the sale of other technologies. Marglin also challenges the sociobiology argument that culture is the product of the "selfish gene":

> If the only certainty about the future is that the future is uncertain,
> if the only sure thing is that we are in for surprises, then no amount
> of planning, no amount of prescription, can deal with the contin-
> gencies that the future will reveal. That is why ultimately there can
> be no agriculture for the people that is not agriculture of the people,

agriculture by the people. People's knowledge developed over centuries, even millennia, is the most important safeguard against disas-
ter and the most sure basis of a resilient, adaptive agriculture. For
this reason, diversity is as necessary to our development as human
beings as it is to ecological balance. Diversity may indeed be the key
to the survival of the human species. Just as exotic species like the
snail darter maintain the diversity of the gene-pool, so does a variety
of practices maintain the diversity of forms of understanding, creating, and coping that the human species has managed to generate.
But within the human species, culture rather than instinct bears the
primary load of intergenerational transmission of knowledge. So the
necessary diversity must be cultural rather than biological. (P. 241)

## *Mythopoetic Narratives and Moral Authority*

If the evolutionary argument is correct, my concerns would be entirely irrelevant. To paraphrase Kelly (1994), we should not be surprised that Nature, having subjugated the bulk of inert matter on
Earth, would go on to subjugate the mythopoetic narratives that
are the basis of the moral codes that constitute this still culturally diverse world. Nature would thus bring them "under its reign of constant evolution, perpetual novelty, and an agenda out of our control"
(p. 471). Since the vast majority of the world's population has not
read the writings of sociobiologists, they are not likely to abandon,
as out of their control, the mythopoetic narratives that frame their
understanding of themselves and their world. Buddhist cultures will
continue to be Buddhist; Muslim cultures will continue to be Muslim; Hindu cultures will continue to be Hindu; and the hundreds
of other cultures whose mythopoetic foundations have their own
distinct origins will continue to be intergenerationally shared and
renewed.

The mythopoetic narratives that are central to Western modernity will continue to make inroads in these cultures—particularly

among the younger generation that watches television and uses the Internet. In addition, the elite in these cultures who have been exposed to Western education will continue to promote Western values and ways of thinking. The acceptance of the metaphorical language of modernity—"development," "progress," "individualism," "freedom," and so forth—on the assumption that such language is objective and does not perpetuate the root metaphors of a specific cultural epistemology, contributes greatly to undermining the substantive symbolic foundations of the world's diverse cultures.

Further, as transnational corporations employ the "survival-of-the-fittest" logic to propagate themselves and undermine traditional cultures, and as the earth's population pushes ecosystems beyond the limits of self-renewal, the question of whether moral values have any basis beyond individual subjective judgment becomes increasingly important. The sociobiologists might argue that there is a gene that regulates consumer behavior, and that gene can be altered. As the technology that accompanies the sociobiologists argument is itself part of the commodification process, the solution to the impact that consumerism has on the environment is not likely to come about by changing human genetic makeup.

The question is whether we can successfully live on this increasingly crowded planet by adopting the moral basis of authority reinforced in the culture of cyberspace. This question is not asked by Turkle, Negroponte, Kelly, or other computer futurists; nor is it asked by sociobiologists and scientists who argue that scientific inquiry leads to the only reliable form of knowledge. Their assumption is that change, even profound changes caused by introducing theoretically based ideas and values into the deep symbolic foundations of a culture, is inherently progressive and thus necessary. Like other Western modern thinkers, they also share the overly simplistic and ethnocentric view of tradition (particularly those of non-Western cultures) as backward and even barbaric—and thus tend to view the spread of modernization as lifting these cultures to a higher level of existence.

The spread of modernization, whether as the Western metanarratives of science (which includes the hubris expressed in Sagan's interpretation), the culture of cyberspace, or the marriage of liberalism with the latest expression of the Industrial Revolution, also promotes secularism and individual moral relativism. Unfortunately, this cultural experiment with communities based on moral reciprocity has not been part of the discussion of a global economic system.

Again, the case for maintaining cultural diversity, even among non-Western cultures we don't understand, is based on the historical evidence of how many of the world's cultures developed relationships and responsibilities that contribute to the quality of life. Gustavo Esteva (1996), for example, cites the example of indigenous cultures that do not punish a murderer in the way that would occur in the West (imprisonment or even execution), but forces the murderer to assume the economic responsibilities of the dead person's family. Indigenous cultures have also developed complex moral codes that regulate relationships with Nature that are not exploitative and reduced to "natural resources." They may be hierarchically organized and retain other patterns that do not meet Western standards of social justice; but they also have avoided the breakdown of the Western family, the growing separation of rich from the poor, drug addiction, and the need to imprison a significant percentage of its minority population.

Clearly, a strong case can be made that many of these cultures need to abandon or revise their traditions. But whether they should be encouraged, mesmerized, or economically blackmailed into accepting the individualistic morality that accompanies modernization, the subjectivity of cyberspace, and the dominant metanarrative of Western science, is indeed problematic. The cultural experiment of mixing individualism and social commodification is proving more costly than even relatively affluent countries can afford. How are the less affluent cultures going to meet the costs of medical treatment, prisons, and other institutionalized attempts to repair social bonds that were not broken to begin with? Many of these cultures are barely coping with the needs of their expanding urban populations. Our modern cultural experiment has harmed the environment much more than the impact of cultures that make community relationships a more central concern than technological and market-oriented activities. While Westerners are accustomed to shopping malls that communicate the cultural message of plenitude and the need for more consumerism, the ultimate test continues to be whether the moral authority of other cultures provide a community existence that limits the adverse impact on the earth's ecosystems. With the growing evidence that corporations are turning the Internet into a worldwide electronic advertising and shopping mall, the advocates of a globalized computer-based culture cannot meet this test.

## *The Metanarrative of Evolution and the Authority of Science*

While computer advocates are explaining the future direction of cultural evolution (as if there were a common future), scientists are increasingly crossing over the line that separates legitimate scientific inquiry from cultural prescriptions, including social engineering. In *Higher Superstition: The Academic Left and Its Quarrels with Science* (1994), Paul R. Gross and Norman Levitt state, "Science is, above all else, a reality-driven enterprise." In this statement we find both the hubris and naiveté expressed in Negroponte's announcement that "computing is not computing anymore. It is about living" (1995, p. 6). Gross and Levitt go on to state the criteria that must be met when investigating the "interplay of cultural and social factors with the workings of scientific research." It is particularly relevant to note what is omitted from the intellectual standards that Gross and Levitt claim must be met by anyone discussing the "interplay" of culture and science:

> Above all . . . it requires an intimate appreciation of the science in question, of its inner logic and of the store of data on which it relies, of its intellectual and experimental tools. In saying this, we are plainly aware that we are setting very high standards for the successful pursuit of such work. We are saying, in effect, that a scholar devoted to a project of this kind must be, *inter alia,* a scientist of professional competence, or nearly so. (Pp. 234–235)

This statement is important for two reasons. First, it asserts that only scientists are qualified to speak or write on the exceedingly complex connections between culture and science. Second, it does not specify the need for the scientist to possess a similar in-depth knowledge of the cultural part of the relationship. The latter becomes especially complex when the differences in cultural traditions and ways of knowing are taken into account.

Readers may think that my concern—the failure of most scientists to recognize that their area of expertise does not qualify them to address cultural issues—does not apply to environmentally oriented scientists. The validity of my concern can be seen in the 1993 message of the Union of Concerned Scientists on the state of the earth's ecosystems. As the cultural aspects of the crisis were totally ignored, the document that was signed by fifteen hundred scientists from around the world framed the solution to reversing the degraded condition of natural systems as essentially a scientific project.

Yet another example of cultural myopia (particularly the reasons why different cultures have vastly different ecological footprints) can be found in the following statement by Martin W. Lewis (1996), who is associated with the program in Comparative Area Studies at Duke University:

> As a self-professed environmentalist, I fully concur that the passage into the twenty-first century sees the world in a state of ecological crisis. I further agree that much of the blame must be assigned to technologies that owe their existence to the success of Enlightenment thought. But I am also convinced that a wholehearted commitment to reason and science offers the only way out of the dilemma. *Only through scientific investigation can we know the origin and magnitude of the planet's problems.* But of equal significance is the fact that only through science can we devise less harmful technologies that will allow us to continue to enjoy the fruits of modernity—which twentieth-century humans will not forswear, no matter how urgent the pleading—without undercutting natural systems in the process. (P. 210, italics added)

To reiterate the pith of his statement: only science can reveal both the origin and extent of the ecological crisis, and only through science will we find the technological solutions that will allow the cultural agenda of modernity to continue.

While these statements purport to be about the legitimate role of scientists, they are examples of scientists crossing the line into discourse over cultural, moral, and political issues. Few scientists have reflected publicly on the connections between Sagan's description of the self-correcting characteristics of scientific inquiry and the cultural assumptions that underlie both liberal ideologies and the Industrial Revolution. Nor have they reflected on how the metanarratives of science contribute to the spread of nihilism—which is largely hidden by the myths of progress and individual self-determination. Most scientists today recognize the questionable morality of the Tuskegee Experiment and the less widely publicized experiments with soldiers and prisoners who unknowingly volunteered to be exposed to radiation. But few speak out today when their colleagues formulate subnarratives that cast scientists in the role of social engineers. For example, Francis Crick's claims that "the aim of science is to explain all aspects of the behavior of our brains, including those of musicians, mystics, and mathematicians" (1994, p. 259), and that our minds can be "explained by the interactions of nerve cells" (p. 7), reflect the engineering mentality that ignores the cultural basis of intelligence and moral judgment. This gross exaggeration of the explanatory power of science, as well as the political dangers connected with this reductionist way of thinking, did not evoke a critical response within the scientific community.

The subnarratives of Moravec and Stock (both educated in highly specialized fields of science) also cast scientists in the critical role of further advancing the technologies that will lead the world to a higher evolutionary stage of monoculture. The new understandings and technologies emerging from the Human Genome Project, for example, are leading to new culturally biased definitions of normality and abnormality, and thus to the ability and right of certain groups to control, by their standards, individuals who supposedly possess "abnormal" or "defective" genes. Wilson and other scientists who subscribe to the argument "genes make individuals" and thus determine the survival traits of cultures, are giving scientists special responsibility for determining the future course of cultural "evolution." Indeed, Wilson urges scientists to recognize their unique historical responsibility to shape the future evolution of humankind. In the book that addresses culture most directly, *On Human Nature* (1978), Wilson acknowledges that the theory of evolution is an epic, even mythopoetic narrative. The following passages reveal the combination of Western hubris and cultural myopia. These passages also reiterate the argument that scientists possess the only reliable knowledge for guiding the future of human evolution—which means, according to the sociobiology argument, that they are the "genetically fittest" and that Nature has chosen to do the work of natural selection through them:

> What I am suggesting, in the end, is that the evolutionary epic is probably the best myth we will ever have. It can be adjusted until it comes as close to the truth as the human mind is constructed to judge the truth. And if that is the case, the mythopoetic requirements of the mind must somehow be met by scientific materialism so as to reinforce our superb energies. . . . In order to address the central issues of the humanities, including ideology and religious belief, science itself must become more sophisticated and in part specially crafted to deal with the peculiar features of human biology. (Pp. 201, 204)

In addressing how science can manage the problem of religious belief, which he describes as "programmed predispositions whose self-sufficient components were incorporated in the neural apparatus of the brain by thousands of generations of genetic evolution" (p. 206), Wilson goes on to urge that "scientific materialism must accommodate (religious belief) on two levels: as a scientific puzzle of great complexity and interest, and as a source of energy that can be shifted in new directions when scientific materialism itself is accepted as the more powerful mythology" (p. 207). As if this were not problematic enough, Wilson makes further claims:

> [This] transition will proceed at an accelerating rate. Man's destiny is to know, if only because societies with knowledge culturally dominate societies that lack it. Luddites and anti-intellectuals do not master the differential equations of thermodynamics or the biochemical cures of illness. They stay in thatched huts and die young. Cultures with unifying goals will learn more rapidly than those which lack them, and an autocatalytic growth of learning will follow because scientific materialism is the only mythology that can manufacture great goals from the sustained pursuit of pure knowledge. (P. 207)

While I am tempted to ask whether Wilson's lack of understanding or evident racism reflects the "programmed predispositions incorporated into the neural apparatus [of his] brain by thousands of generations of genetic evolution," I want to include a quote that demonstrates the danger of scientists using their special area of scientific knowledge for predicting the future pathway of "evolution" that all cultures are to follow. The privileged role of scientists for guiding human evolution is summed up in a way that is highly messianic:

> The true Promethean spirit of science means to liberate man by giving him knowledge and some measure of dominion over the physical environment. But on another level, and in a new age, it also constructs the mythology of scientific materialism, guided by the corrective devices of the scientific method, addressed with precise and deliberately affective appeal to the deepest needs of human nature, and kept strong by the blind hopes that the journey on which we are now embarked will be farther and better than the one just completed. (P. 209)

In *Consilience: The Unity of Knowledge* (1998), Wilson again attempts to explain why all areas of human inquiry (in all cultures) need to be grounded in an understanding of how thought, values, behavior, and other expressions of culture develop "under the joint influence of heredity and environment." Here, Wilson understands heredity as more than the genetic orchestration of chemical processes that determine a person's physical and mental characteristics; it also must be understood in terms of whether the genes possess superior Darwinian fitness—which means the ability of future generations to survive. Wilson's deep concern is that the nonindustrial cultures' continued reliance on prescientific thinking will destroy the support systems in the environment that humans depend on. This leads him to reiterate his way of averting the crisis he sees immediately ahead: "evolution, including genetic progress in human nature and human capacity, will be from now on increasingly the domain of science and technology tempered by ethics and political choice" (p. 277). The latter, of course, are also the expression of genetic-cultural coevolution—which, again, scientists are best qualified to understand. Given the varied political agendas that scientists have supported since the beginning of the Industrial Revolution, Wilson's extrapolation of evolution theory to sanction scientific responsibility for the future development of all the world's cultures points to yet another danger of embedding our understanding of computers in the scientific metanarrative of evolution. Wilson continually stresses cooperation as an adaptive trait of individuals and cultures, but other readings of the scientist's Rosetta stone stress that "genetic fitness" is determined through competition. This is the message of evolutionary biology that computer industry leaders have seen confirmed in their industry: only the strongest competitors survive. Thus, they will continue to use the message as justification for making other cultures dependent on computer technology.

I doubt that many people who rely on computers for their knowledge would be able to recognize when scientists cross the line that separates competent and informed judgments from inadequately informed efforts to speak and write as experts on cultural matters. There is another question that needs to be raised about the educational influence of computers. It has very different implications from that of being able to think critically about the formation of new cultural myths, especially myths that give special authority to an elite group who possesses powerful technologies that supposedly do not require a deep understanding of different cultures and how these differences in ways of knowing impact the natural environment. The question is whether the vocabulary for naming (and thus recognizing) the differences between cultural traditions that contribute to viable community and environmental relationships can be learned without the intergenerational communication that computers now undermine. Questions about the efficacy of computer-mediated learning also need to take account of the relativizing and "ever-in-process" individual subjectivity that Turkle views as one of the major advantages of cyberspace.

With Silicon Valley generating sales of more than $200 billion a year, and other regions of the world competing to develop their own cyberspace-connected economies, it is unlikely that the discussion of these questions will come from within the computer industry. Nor is it likely to come from within those in the scientific community who view themselves as Nature's chosen people. Whether this discussion can emerge from the margins of the academic community is also doubtful. But as I am still somewhat optimistic, the following chapters will address the responsibility of public school teachers and university professors for providing a more critical understanding of the cultural mediating characteristics of computers. This will lead to questioning the underlying cultural assumptions that have made the public so eager to embrace a technology and the legitimating evolutionary ideology that are undermining the forms of knowledge and intergenerational communication so essential for living less consumer-dependent and thus less environmentally destructive lives.

These assumptions must be examined in light of the issues raised in this chapter: (1) the way in which the scientific metanarrative of evolution is invoked to justify the spread of computer-based technologies has, as one of its side effects, the further depoliticization of technological decision making; (2) the growing influence of scientists and technocrats who are working to create a world monoculture that is undermining the sustaining capacity of natural systems; (3) the importance of conserving culturally diverse traditions of local knowledge that have enabled groups to develop technologies and systems of mutual support that take account of their bioregions; and (4) the need to understand the forms of noncommercialized relationships, knowledge, and skills that still exist among cultural groups living in urban and rural America. A more complex understanding of the latter two issues is essential to recognizing the appropriate and inappropriate uses of computers. It will also help in clarifying the limits of scientific knowledge and the danger of undermining the symbolic foundations of the moral systems of other cultures.

# *Part 2*
# Educational Consequences

The optimism that pervades the way computers are represented to the public is genuine. It would be wrong to criticize the writings of Turkle, Negroponte, Kelly, Papert, and others as containing deliberate half-truths concocted to sell more computers. The problem is not crass commercialism; it is more a surprisingly superficial understanding of the culturally transformative quality of computers. The failure of the computer proponents is in not asking more probing questions about the forms of knowledge that computers cannot process and in not examining the deep cultural assumptions that give their thinking such an ethnocentric and formulaic quality.

At deeper fault is our educational system, which fails to provide computer proponents and their followers with an understanding of the complex relationship between culture and technology. This failure also accounts for the general public's inability to recognize that not all technological innovations are expressions of progress. If public schools and universities were providing the education that a technologically influenced democracy needs, instead of catering to the educational agenda desired by corporations, then we the public would be better able to articulate and debate relevant issues before a new technology was incorporated into the web of seemingly irreversible dependencies.

The following chapters look at how educators understand the potential of computers and at the cultural values reinforced through both computers and software programs. We will see how the thinking of leading computer proponents mirrors their silences and misunderstandings.

# 5 The False Promises of Computer-Based Education

The national media are raising doubts about computers as an antidote to our systemic educational shortcomings. While some in academia had questioned the apparent educational gains of computers, their books were viewed as out of touch with the euphoria created by the computer industry's heavily financed promotions and by professors who saw new career paths for themselves. Reservation from classroom teachers, which mostly took the form of passive resistance, similarly had no influence on school boards or on a computer industry determined to carry out the technological revolution essential to the Age of Information. Todd Oppenheimer's article, "The Computer Delusion," which appeared in the July 1997 issue of the *Atlantic Monthly*, contained interviews and other anecdotal evidence showing that, in spite of the huge expenditures on computers for classroom use, the hoped-for gains have not been realized. The article presented a picture of educational misuses, false promises, and distorted funding priorities. It even suggested that cutting school subjects and other curricular resources in order to acquire more computers in the classroom "may be educational malpractice."

But the national visibility critics are now receiving does not represent a shift in the priorities of politicians, educational decision makers, or a computer industry still determined to exploit the full market potential of public schools and universities. Leading politicians continue to thwart genuine national debate by equating prosperity with computers, including classroom computers. President Clinton, for example, made computers in public school classrooms an essential component to his "bridge to the twenty-first century." The cost of achieving the universal computer competency he envisioned was estimated between $40 and $100 billion from 1998 to 2003. Other politicians have been equally quick to embrace computers as the panacea for addressing the nation's most intractable problems. The former Speaker of the House, Newt Gingrich, promoted the idea that giving laptops to the poor will alleviate their plight, while Al Gore continues to argue that preparation for the future requires that computers be given a more central role in education. Politicians at all levels of government have embraced the new mythology that equates information with individual empowerment and economic well-being. The computer industry's increasing courtship of politicians has also been an important source of influence. With so many dollars at stake, politicians are not likely to challenge the growing dependency on computer-based technologies—even if they understand the underlying cultural, political, and moral issues involved.

Dependence on computers is growing in all areas of public school and university activity. Witness the increasing number of public school students "plugged into" computers (ten students for every computer in 1997, compared to twenty-five students sharing one computer 1989). Witness too the increasing reliance on e-mail for student-professor communication, the shift to virtual libraries, and the growing number of courses offered in cyberspace (a trend we shall examine later in more depth). That computers represent the hallmark of progress and are thus the cornerstone of the educational process is a belief that is spreading, like a cultural virus, to other parts of the world. The obstacles to making computer-mediated learning the basis of educational reform are more economic than cultural.

In North America, proponents of "technology-rich education," as one computer consultant put it, have clearly controlled the discussion of educational reform by promising endless educational gains and by enforcing in public consciousness the belief that classroom computers are the key to future prosperity. Criticism of computer-mediated learning, on the other hand, focuses typically on the following concerns: (1) computers limit students' imagination; (2) computer advocates overstate the connection between data and thinking; (3) students often have only a superficial understanding of the information they download; (4) computers frequently break down; (5) underfunded schools have less access to computers and thus put already disenfranchised students at further disadvantage; (6) computer-based learning has negative physical side effects that we are just beginning to understand.

These criticisms are partly valid, but they do not illuminate the deeper intrinsic limitations of computer-based education. The current criticism lacks a global perspective on the cultural roots of our ecological crisis. With the exception of Langdon Winner (1986), Jerry Mander (1991), and Theodore Roszak, I cannot think of any critic, even among those who should be taken seriously for other reasons, who integrates a cultural-ecological perspective. In *The Cult of Information* (1994), Theodore Roszak examines how computers reinforce Cartesian thinking, but his comparison is between traditional and contemporary ways of thinking in the West. He also uses the Luddite analogy to argue that computers will have a similar impact on the remaining self-sufficient capacities of today's communities. What is missing is how the Western technological mind-set differs from that of other cultural groups—particularly those that have encoded their knowledge of place, relationships, and life cycles into their mentoring, narratives, and ceremonies.

The experience of a local school district in a Northwest city is typical of how school districts across the country regard economic globalization in relation (or not) to the global ecological crisis. Following a statewide property tax revolt similar to California's Proposition 13, the district was forced to lay off teachers and administrators. At the same time, it passed a local bond measure that provided funds to purchase two thousand computers and corresponding Internet wiring for classrooms. The capital expenditure required a computer maintenance budget of $80,000 per year, plus the salary for three technical staff who keep the equipment repaired. As these computers will soon need to be upgraded or entirely replaced to keep current with industry innovations, the district faces yet another major expenditure within a few years. The social pressures that led to the purchase and wiring decisions explain why the debate on computers is so one-sided and conceptually limited.

At the time the investment decision was made, there were a few letters to the editor of the local newspaper questioning why music and art classes were being dropped from the curriculum. There were also questions raised at school board meetings. But they were overwhelmed by those who argued that computer-based learning would not only represent a vast improvement over traditional educational approaches but would also prepare students for the twenty-first-century workplace.

Teachers in the district who had taken computer education courses at the local university had already been exposed to systematic pro-tech arguments for computers in the classroom. The statewide media continually highlighted how the high-tech companies moving into the state were transforming the economy. In addition, as more computers were placed in schools, a computer specialist was assigned to each school to serve as chief technological advocate among the teachers. Consequently, teachers who could articulate what is educationally problematic about computers were not accorded special status within the school. The local business community and the computer giants crowding into the state's "Silicon Forest" also contributed to the growing consensus that computers represent the most intelligent educational investment for achieving a big economic payoff in the future. With Intel donating memory boards to local school districts, who would suggest that teachers should follow an alternative pathway of cultural development?

The rush to embrace this educationally unproven technology was furthered by parents who either were indifferent to educational priorities or were committed to introducing their children to computers at the earliest possible age by acquiring a computer for the home.

## Framing Computer Use in Schools: National Approaches

In recent years it has been difficult to find an article or interview in prestigious newspapers, popular magazines, or academic journals that does not praise the educational advantages of computers. The following examples taken from a wide variety of print media are typical. Seymour Papert, the author of *Mindstorms: Children, Computers, and Powerful Ideas* (1980) and, more recently, *The Connected Family: Bridging the Digital Generation Gap* (1996), is perhaps the most influential and widely interviewed proponent of computer-mediated learning. In an interview that appeared in the *Christian Science Monitor* (de Pommereau, 1997), Papert expressed his optimism about the coming educational revolution when he claimed, "Never before has a society been so close to freeing children from school walls, grading systems, and overdependence upon adults" (p. 11). In an interview that appeared in the *San Francisco Chronicle* (Evenson, 1997), Papert stated that "our goal in education should be to foster the ability to use computers in everything we do, even if you don't have a specific piece of software for the job" (section 3, p. 3). He also restated what has become an educational mantra: "Teachers should not be dispensers of knowledge, but guides on the side."

Alan C. Kay made a similar claim in an article that appeared in *Scientific American* (Kay, 1991). However, he framed it as meeting the challenge of moving beyond the predispositions of our "biology to live in the barbarisms of the deep past." Using an argument that is widely promoted in teacher education programs and popular among postmodern thinkers, Kay claimed that "each of us has to construct our own version of reality by main force, literally to make ourselves. And we are quite capable of devising new mental bricks, new ways of thinking, that can enormously expand the understandings we attain. The bricks we develop become new technologies for thinking" (1991, p. 140).

The claims made in professional publications are even more specific about the educational gains. In an article that appeared in the *Chronicle of Higher Education* (which publishes a weekly article on the various educational benefits of computers), David L. Wilson explained how hypertext could revolutionize teaching: "A hypertext tome . . . allows each reader to control how the work is read. By choosing their own paths through the work—pointing and clicking on whatever strikes their interest—readers impose on the work their own version of linearity, sometimes in ways the author never intended" (1997, p. A25). Mike Muir presented a similar argument in an article that appeared in *Educational Leadership* (Muir, 1994), the journal most widely read by classroom teachers and administrators. In the article titled "Putting Computer Projects at the Heart of the Curriculum," Muir restates the widely held assumption that computers facilitate the natural process of learning disrupted in the past by authoritarian ways of thinking about the student-teacher relationship:

> We know that students learn by constructing their own knowledge through using information in meaningful ways. This new knowledge must be built directly on what each student already knows, and the student must see the connection between the new ideas and their world. Further, students need to be actively involved in their own learning and the decisions about learning. To achieve this, we decided to make computers a part of the school infrastructure. (P. 30)

Even educational theorists who consider themselves leading interpreters of how to achieve a more egalitarian and just society are viewing computers as a liberation technology. In explaining how the Internet can be used to foster collaborative critical inquiry in the classroom, Jim Cummins and Dennis Sayers (1997) reiterate the main argument of the computer industry: learning to use the Internet will lead to a more innovative and productive workforce better able to manipulate information. While they argue that marginalized social groups need to have equal access to computer-mediated learning, their vision of a more egalitarian society includes both fuller participation of all groups in the civic life of the community and "greater financial assets, which will spur consumption and further production" (p. 177).

Two Australian educational theorists view the emancipatory potential of cyberspace in even more optimistic terms. In a statement that reflects the assumption that computers are a neutral tool and that their socially constructive or destructive potential depends on who controls them, Michael Peters and Colin Lankshear (1996) make the following claim:

> From the standpoint of educational values and aims, at least some—and perhaps much—of the experimentation and creativity evident in the development of new vocabularies, signs, and codes by cyberspace citizens testifies to a human will to activity, invention, and transformative engagement which resists logics of scarcity, ownership, and even, perhaps, profits. . . . [T]his participatory and interactive medium potentially offers new accessibility to the power to inform and be informed: not as a commodity or fixed possession bought and sold under the logic of exchange value. (P. 64)

Peters and Lankshear fail to understand that computer-mediated communication, by its nature, involves a commodified relationship—even in its most interactive forms of expression. Second, the characteristics of "cyberspace citizens" represent the most extreme individualism at the heart of Western liberalism—creative, experimental, emancipated from traditions, and supposedly altruistic enough to use power only for the betterment of humanity. In short, their vision of computer-based empowerment rests on a surprisingly superficial understanding of the cultural form of subjectivity reinforced by computers.

As cultural critique is not usually a strength of high-level politicians, we must evaluate differently the promises used to promote a "Western virtual university." The idea of meeting the growing demand for higher education in Western states by building a virtual university emerged from a 1995 meeting of the governors of eleven Western states. Not only was the idea justified on technological grounds, it also was seen as solving other concerns. Establishing a virtual university would eliminate the heavy financial burden of building new campuses and hiring faculty that, under the present system of tenure, represent a long-term economic commitment. In addition, the virtual university would eliminate courses and degree requirements that reflect different academic disciplines rather than the current needs of the workplace. In effect, the virtual university was seen as offering an inexpensive delivery system while marginalizing the gatekeeper role of more critically minded academics who might pose a political threat.

As the planning team of the Western Governors' University (as it was first known) envisioned it, the often uneasy relationship between certain segments of the university and the business community would become a thing of the past. Internet-based courses would cultivate the competencies that fit the changing needs of employers, while course evaluations and degree certification would demand demonstration of required competencies. Moreover, students would be free of the restrictions of traditional academic schedules and the extra expense connected with taking courses on a university campus. Students would also have greater responsibility for assessing the knowledge and competencies they most need and, with the aid of a cyberspace counselor, decide which courses would best prepare them for the changing workplace. According to one promotional statement, the challenge facing higher education in the Information Age is to provide "just-in-time" learning for employees.

The press releases and promotional literature overlook the traditional purposes associated with higher education: the advancement of knowledge, the exposure to a broad range of cultural traditions that enable active and reflective participation in civic life, the development of personal talents, and so forth. Instead, the metaphorical language of the business community extols the "New System of Learning for the Cybercentury." Examples include the metaphor of the marketplace to frame the three primary roles of the virtual university and the explanation that "delivery system" costs would be kept low through "outsourcing" courses to public and private "providers." In addition, the potential of the virtual university as "a major force in the distant learning market" would "generate substantial cash flow," thus further reducing the states' traditional economic burden.

However, these expectations were not realized. During the academic year 1998–1999, after one year of operation and a start-up cost of over $13 million, only 120 students enrolled in courses offered by the thirty-nine colleges and universities now affiliated with the Western Governors' University, and only 100 students enrolled in the unaccredited degree programs. With this cyberspace approach to higher education needing 3,000 students enrolled in degree programs to meet operating costs, Apple, IBM, Microsoft, and America Online are being asked to make up the financial shortfall.

While the literature describing the Western virtual university strongly implies that it is on the cutting edge of emerging technological and educational innovation, many universities across the country already have been offering courses, and even entire degree programs, over various two-way interactive networks and, more recently, the Internet. For example, the Michigan Information Technology Network, a partnership of educational, public, and business organizations, offers graduate degrees in fifteen disciplines. Other universities, such as the sixty-four-campus State University of New York, Texas A&M, and Pennsylvania State University view the vast potential of the "distant learning market" as both a welcome source of income and a threat to many of the traditions associated with campus-based learning. In an article that appeared in the *Chronicle of Higher Education* under the title "Extending the Reach of Virtual Classrooms," Robert L. Jacobson (1994) summarized the questions that the new technologies were raising for the academic community:

> How will distance-learning courses affect faculty workloads and compensation? How much help or supplementary pay should a professor receive, for example, if the course he or she is teaching to 30 students in one classroom also engages several hundred other students at distant sites? Do instructors merit special consideration if they're regularly swapping electronic mail with hundreds of students instead of simply scheduling a few office hours each week? (Pp. A20–22)

These questions reflect concerns about the economic dislocations, including job security issues, that most proponents of educational computing fail to mention. More important, they reflect the growing moral and conceptual relativism within the academic community that has resulted in replacing consensus on essential forms of knowledge with concerns about equitable working conditions. Not that campuswide debates on the Western canon and liberal education lend moral and conceptual clarity to the environmental issues we now face—they do not. Rather, the emphasis on job security issues indicates the difficulty that lies ahead in getting the academic community to question the culturally transformative effects of computers.

Not even the concern with job security has reversed a trend that is spreading across the country. Using a computer program called Web Course Tools, the entire faculty at UCLA, following a decision mandated by the university administration, are putting their courses on-line. The web page for the one thousand courses offered each term contains the basic information about course purpose, content, and readings. Professors are expected to add audio and video clips, lecture notes, and anything else relevant to the course. The web page also has a discussion area that allows students to "chat" with each other and with the professor. The advantages for administrators and the disadvantages for professors of putting courses on-line can be more clearly seen in the case of the New School in New York City. Administrators are hiring mostly unemployed academics with Ph.D. degrees to design on-line courses, with the understanding that the university owns all rights to the course. The university pays the "teachers" a flat fee and saves the cost of a regular faculty salary (Noble, 1998). The next step Educom (the academic corporate consortium) is pursuing is to standardize course content and evaluation so they can be processed by computer-based network systems. This digitized industrial model of university education is estimated to represent a market of over $200 billion for such corporate giants as AT&T, IBM, and Macintosh.

Unfortunately, what Noble calls the corporate-regulated "diploma mill" will have consequences that go beyond this latest development in the commodification of knowledge and relationships between students and professors. One particularly serious consequence is that the new secular trinity of education, computers, and the marketplace exacerbates a double bind: while computers enable near-instantaneous communication between corporate power centers and production facilities in different parts of the world and integrate low-wage countries into the global economy, they further undermine the traditional connections between education and job security. The current emphasis on tailoring public school and university curricula to fit the changing needs of the workplace ignores how computers not only contribute to the accelerating rate of technological change but also enable the rapid relocation of production facilities to areas of the world where labor costs are lowest. The increased linkage between education and computers contributes to a growing instability that is psychologically and economically costly for individuals, families, and communities—but has tangible economic benefits for computer-oriented educators. The sooner skills and knowledge are made obsolete, the more the educational market expands as part of the retraining process—thus benefiting virtual universities and other educational "providers." The procomputer arguments can be faulted for reflecting a combination of unexamined cultural assumptions, abstract thinking reinforced by spending too much time in cyberspace, and a dangerous combination of altruism and romanticism. We should not overlook how these arguments mask a more basic concern with power and economic gain.

This expansion of the educational market is but a stepping-stone to a time when computer-based technologies replace classroom teachers. The recent introduction of a software program that can grade essays suggests that even the ability to recognize thoughtful analysis and graceful writing does not make teachers immune to technological displacement.

The public's inability to engage in a national debate on computers can be traced back to the one-sided approach of educational institutions: they have supported computer proliferation but ignored the public's need to weigh the increased vulnerability of their life-sustaining symbolic infrastructure against the gains accrued to the few. This approach has narrowed both the educational and political process to the point where few individuals can imagine viable alternatives.

## Educational Software: Who Is Responsible for Cultural Content?

In the *Cult of Information* (1994), Theodore Roszak makes an insightful observation that escaped the attention of both proponents and critics of classroom computers. For students sitting in front of a computer screen, moving a cursor, and accessing data, the fundamental relationship is not between them and their machines. Rather, it is between the mind of the student and the minds of the people who designed the mechanical systems of the computer and who wrote the software that contains the conceptual matrix within which students think. As I put it in *The Cultural Dimensions of Educational Computing* (1988), the metaphorical language that appears on the screen frames the thought processes of students as they organize data, make simulated decisions, and do word processing. Martin Heidegger stated this fundamental relationship even more succinctly when he observed that "language already hides within itself a developed way of conceiving" (1962, p. 199). When incorporated within a theory that explains how earlier forms of metaphorical thinking are reproduced in analogic thinking and encoded in iconic metaphors, this insight generally is ignored at all levels of education, from elementary to graduate. As pointed out earlier, the idea of objective knowledge that can be communicated in sender-receiver fashion through language is one of the most deeply held orthodoxies among all educators.

Ironically, the technology that is proclaimed as revolutionizing the deepest foundations of culture is rooted in this basic misunderstanding of language. This misunderstanding partly accounts for one of the most important oversights of computer-mediated learning: the symbol systems appearing on the screen reproduce the implicit thought patterns of the software programmers. The failure of educators to make the cultural content of the software a primary concern can be traced to the curricula of computer education classes and the guidance from "experts" who write the professional journals.

For readers unfamiliar with the low level of discourse about educational computing within universities I provide the following examples of professional guidance offered to teachers and parents. In an article appearing in *MacUser* magazine, Joseph Schorr (1994) identified ten rules parents should follow in choosing educational software for their children (pp. 91–94):

1. Try before you buy
2. Make sure it is fun
3. Insist on interactivity and exploration
4. Make sure interface is "childproof"
5. Think beyond your Mac
6. Get involved—then stay involved
7. One size doesn't fit all
8. Listen to experts
9. Choose content carefully
10. Don't underestimate basic hardware requirements

The rule suggesting that content is an important consideration is explained in terms of the sex and violence themes that responsible parents already consider when judging the appropriateness of movies and books. But competitive decision making, extreme subjectivity, and consumer tendencies are not mentioned as aspects of software content that parents should be concerned about. The "expert" guidance turns out to be little more than the common sense that most thoughtful adults have learned in other areas of responsible parenting.

As I point out in *The Culture of Denial* (1997), the emphasis on technique, process, and application that characterizes most professional literature on computer-mediated learning traces back to the educational background of professors of education, and further back to their professors. With few exceptions, their education never cultivated an appreciation of differences in cultural ways of knowing, an understanding of metaphorical language and cultural intelligence, or even the cultural mediating characteristics of print-based technologies such as computers. As a result, university "experts" on educational computing, with few exceptions, are unable to see, much less explain, cultural nuances and teachers' responsibilities for safeguarding them. Nor can these experts see the cultural assumptions embedded in software programs. Given this lack of understanding, they cannot convey to teachers the connections between the tacit and explicit cultural ways of thinking that contribute to global warming and other environmental degradations.

In 1985 when I was doing the background research for writing *The Cultural Dimensions of Educational Computing,* I was surprised by the number of textbooks and professional journals that provided little more than an explanation of the different strategies for using computers in the classroom. Little has changed since then. For example, in an article titled "Is It Too Late to Offer Introductory Computer Workshops to Faculty and Staff?" Leigh E. Zeitz (1996) reproduces the same explanation that was prevalent fifteen years ago. After providing his readers with an affirmative answer, he nevertheless devotes the rest of the article to explaining the concepts that should be covered in the workshop: understanding the differences between a floppy and a hard disk; between an operating system and a program; and between the graphic user interface environments Mac and DOS. Zeitz also explains the best way to overcome teacher anxiety about using the mouse. Like many other publications, the article introduces teachers to computer vocabulary, but it fails to mention the distinctive characteristics of computers that directly relate to the teacher's responsibility in the primary socialization that students undergo when using a computer. Zeitz's explanations might contribute to teachers' mechanical literacy but not their ability to recognize the cultural mediating characteristics of computers—which is essential to helping students understand potential uses and misuses of the technology. Teachers taking Zeitz's workshop will not learn the differences between an electronic and a face-to-face community, nor will they understand that data and information are objectified interpretations that, in turn, are based on a culturally specific pattern of thinking.

The same is true for contemporary textbooks. The authors of *Instructional Technology for Teaching and Learning* (Newby, Stepich, Lehman, and Russell, 1996) offer the following vision of the direction educational reform will take:

> We envision a future where teachers and learners embrace and integrate instructional technology and use it to improve the teaching and learning process. . . . Here are some of the things we see as possible outcomes of this process: multimedia learning resources, available via information networks, will proliferate and become a central feature of education. Teachers will change their role from the "sage on the stage" to the "guide on the side." Instead of conveying information, they will help learners make use of the new information tools to find, analyze, and synthesize information; to solve problems; to think creatively; and to construct their own understanding. Education will become a lifelong process, one that is important and accessible to all, and schools will become centers of learning—not just for children but for all members of the community. The boundaries separating schools from each other and from the community will blur or disappear. (P. 330)

This summary contains all the unexamined and unproven assumptions the promotional literature aims at a credulous general public to secure hope for the technological future. The sense of linear, technological progress, the belief that computers are part of the evolution toward a new digitized global culture, the assumptions that individuals construct their own knowledge and determine their own values and that data and information are the basis of thinking, are presented as the insights of futuristic thinkers. For individuals who have read other educational computing textbooks and articles, the promises are the all-too-familiar litany of professional optimism that reflects a basic ignorance of how language and computers influence culture. In the sections of *Instructional Technology for Teaching and Learning* that explain the three theories of learning (behaviorism, constructivism, and information processing), there is no reference to differences in cultural ways of knowing, nor to the ways the metaphorical language of computers reproduces the cognitive schemata of the dominant cultural group. Given the authors' conceptual orthodoxies, it is easy to understand why teachers and the general public ignore the cultural content of educational software.

When we examine the cultural assumptions, values, and patterns of thinking encountered in educational software, the power of Roszak's insight into the "mind meeting mind" relationship becomes clearer. When many parents and teachers deliberately examine the conceptual and moral frameworks embedded in the facts, information, and decision-making skills software programs cultivate, they are likely to view the software as reinforcing their own implicit assumptions and values and thus be highly supportive. As most educational software reproduces the same cultural patterns experienced as normal in our modern, technological, and consumer-driven society, few middle-class parents and teachers recognize the double binds created by these assumptions and values—particularly how they contribute to ecologically degenerative economic and technological practices. Few parents and teachers will recognize the historical linkages between their highest values (including their own view of personal success) and the Industrial Revolution, with all its ecological implications. For most of us, those connections—between a 7,000-square-mile "dead zone" of oxygenless water that stretches from the mouth of the Mississippi River each summer and our modern view of individualism; between ponds in New England that have not frozen for twenty years due to global warming and our cyber version of creativity; between the chemically saturated, eroded topsoil of the Midwest and our deadly ecological anthropocentrism; between declines in our reproductive capacity and our addiction to consumerism—these connections are difficult to see. Abetting us in our willful blindness are the educational software programs developed by an intellectual elite who continue to promote the deep cultural assumptions that have led to turning Nature and human relationships into commodities.

Until we recognize the connections between computer-mediated learning and the ecologically destructive patterns of its correlating culture, criticism of the assumptions and values being reinforced in educational software will seem reactionary and grossly misdirected. That the education acquired in public schools and universities leaves most people unable to recognize these connections is perhaps the most important issue society faces.

With the hundreds of educational software programs designed for every age group, which range from the "edutainment" format to the growing number of environmentally oriented programs, it is easy to identify egregious instances of violence, racial and gender bias, and gross misinformation that should concern even the most staunch supporters of educational computing. Rather than analyze the weakest programs, I will examine the cultural assumptions and values embedded in programs widely regarded as having the most educational merit—and have even been identified in the *New York Times* as the most outstanding examples of educational software. I will start with a software program, *Storybook Weaver* (1993), intended for students in grades K through 4, and then analyze programs designed for middle and high school students. This progression from early grades through high school will provide a better sense of how ecologically problematic assumptions continue to be reinforced as students reach supposedly higher levels of thinking and more difficult subject areas.

The teacher's manual explaining the educational advantages of *Storybook Weaver* emphasizes the importance of young students having access to a creative "tool" that translates their imagination into publishable stories. One of the features of the program allows students to click on the name of a traditional children's story that can be read like a book. But the main emphasis is on students writing their own stories (supported by the choice of 650 images, 450 scenery combinations, and a wide range of sounds, songs, and page boarder ornaments). Unfortunately, the social need that *Storybook Weaver* intends to fulfill is based on assumptions of individualism that, in lacking collective experience accumulated over generations, depends on consumerism. As the teacher's manual puts it:

> Teachers are faced with the tremendous task of preparing today's students for tomorrow's world—a world characterized by change in an information-rich environment. Thinking skills are at the heart of this thriving, changing environment, for these are the behaviors students most practice in school and continue to apply the rest of their lives. . . . We are confident that you (the teacher) will find *Storybook Weaver* of considerable value in your classroom as you foster student thinking. (P. 47)

The long list of individually centered thinking skills include "comparing," "classifying," "representing," "identifying attributes and components," "inferring," "predicting," "summarizing," and others. Contrary to the way the teacher's manual represents thinking as individualistic, thinking skills are not culturally neutral; they are always framed in terms of background cultural assumptions that students bring to the relationships and events. As stated earlier, these assumptions are learned implicitly as the basis of the conceptual framework for thinking and communicating in the metaphorical language of the student's cultural group.

Like so many of the conceptual orthodoxies held by teachers and software designers, the thinking used to promote *Storybook Weaver* assumes that culturally autonomous students construct their own understanding of the external world. This approach leads to ecologically problematic cultural patterns of thinking. It also is problematic for students who bring a different set of cultural assumptions to the program's matrix of decision making. Given that *Storybook Weaver*'s dominant feature is to reinforce students' subjective judgment, we must consider the educational impact on the student who comes from a culture that encodes its moral framework and knowledge of ecological relationships in the narratives that are passed down through the generations.

*Storybook Weaver* not only encourages the student to make decisions about the storyline but also about the geographical features in which the story will be situated, as well as the animals, plants, and types of buildings that will be part of the visual background. The student's imagination may result in a landscape background where a palm tree sits on an iceberg, with giraffes and other animals nearby that the student may decide to put there. The student may choose to put a castle in the middle of the ocean—if that is the environment that the student wants to create. The 650 images and 450 scenery combinations that the program makes available to the student provide for a wide range of imaginative possibilities. And this is where the real problem arises.

What the creators of *Storybook Weaver* view as the expression of students' creative imagination can also be viewed as extreme anthropocentrism. Rather than a knowledge of specific ecosystems and cultural traditions (architectural styles, clothes, technologies, and so on) the student's subjective experience is the basis of learning. Understanding how animals coevolved within a specific bioregion, knowing how cultural groups historically responded to the particularities of their local environments—contextual knowledge such as this is totally irrelevant. In fact, acquiring such knowledge in a systematic manner would be seen as a constraint on the student's creativity. *Storybook Weaver* reinforces a multidimensional subjectivity that makes geography, botany, zoology, and the histories of different cultural groups dependent on the imagination of six- to ten-year-old students.

*DynoPark Tycoon* (1994), a simulation program aimed at students in grades 4 though 12, not only socializes students to adopt what Jerry Mander calls a Disneyland mentality toward Nature, it also teaches the core values that underlie the commodification process of a global economy. Like *Storybook Weaver*, the program is justified on the grounds that it develops thinking skills such as "estimating," "forecasting," "reading and understanding graphs," and "understanding cause and effect relationships." However, the explanation of the program's educational significance ignores the values and assumptions reinforced in every facet of their main activity: learning to manage the roadside attraction that features life-sized replicas of dinosaurs. In learning how to advertise, set prices, control expenses, and purchase land and equipment, students are also learning how to measure relationships, experiences, and activities in terms of their market value and profit potential. As the simulation does not require students to reflect on which aspects of community life and the natural world should remain immune from the market criteria of profit and loss, students are being further socialized to think of supply and demand as the basic moral guideline for assessing activities and relationships. That other cultures might regard nature as sacred and value morally reciprocal face-to-face relationships over relationships based on economic exchange is totally ignored by the program's designers. Indeed, the cultural mind-set students encounter as they enter the matrix of decision making is identical with the mind-set that provided the energy and moral sense of direction to the Industrial Revolution and to the accompanying process of colonization. The elements of this mind-set include the continual quest for new products and markets, the anthropocentric view of nature as a resource to be consumed for personal gain, and individual exemption from cultural traditions that establish boundaries for moral and immoral relationships.

*DynoPark Tycoon* and *Storybook Weaver* share one more limitation. Because most teachers take for granted the assumptions and values embedded in the program, there is little likelihood those values will be made explicit and put in a historical and comparative cultural perspective. Nor it is likely that students will be encouraged to reflect on the ecological implications of globalizing the values and assumptions they are learning or to consider how they are integral to the spread of Western technologies, including computers.

Perhaps the most popular historical simulation aimed at a student population is *The Oregon Trail II* (1993), for students in grades 5 though 12. The original version was introduced in 1975 and has gone through a number of revisions. The teacher's manual for the latest version lists thirty-one learning objectives, one of which appears especially ironic, considering the biases built into the matrix of decisions available to students: through the program, students will learn to "see things from others' point of view by studying people from the past" (p. 4). Like the formulaic promises that appear to accompany all educational software, there is again no mention of the culturally specific values and ways of thinking reinforced as students engage in simulated decision making. The theory of learning underlying the program is based instead on the naive view of the student's thought process as a series of rational judgments, such as classifying data and ideas in terms of established categories and learning to ask "appropriate and searching questions." The program is designed to give students a number of options for each situation encountered on the trek along the Oregon Trail: students make choices about how to cross a river, where to set up a camp, how to repair broken equipment, and so forth. More important, in deciding among the options made available by the program, students are drawn into the simulated cultural mind-set of the emigrants making their way through the "wilderness" to the Oregon Territory. In effect, the form of intelligence the students are allowed to express is that of the emigrants—including their assumptions about their right to claim and settle the land.

In his insightful critique, "On the Road to Cultural Bias," Bill Bigelow (1995) notes that while women are represented in nearly every scene, the decisions that students re-enact reflect the dominance of the male perspective. Decisions that reflect the issues and values of women, particularly those relating to the everyday challenges and routines of family and community life, are not part of the virtual reality that students enter. For female students, *The Oregon Trail II* fulfills the promise of learning "others' point of view"—but it's the point of view of a male adventure story set in the wild West. He also notes another interesting characteristic of the simulation that relates directly to the cultural points of view students are learning to adopt. In the earlier version, bandits appeared on the screen riding horses and wearing feathers in their headbands. Most students quickly recognized that the bandits were Indians. In later versions, Indians are portrayed in a more politically correct light as friendly sources of information and thus as assistants to the emigrants in their new homelands. In one scene, Indians are shown as reluctant to associate with the emigrants out of a fear of disease. But, as Bigelow observes, the Indians are never represented as hostile. Thus, "despite the increasing violence along the Oregon Trail, the one choice *Oregon Trail II* programmers don't offer students-astrekkers is the choice to harm Indians" (1995, p. 16). The simulated encounters between emigrants and Indians, in effect, distort the students' understanding of the emigrants' view of Indians as culturally inferior and as a potential physical threat that must be continually guarded against.

The later versions of *The Oregon Trail* introduce the names of the Indian tribes encountered on the way to the Oregon Territory. Students are even encouraged to role-play being a Cheyenne child. The teacher's manual suggests that the role-playing exercise will require research and the use of the student's imagination. The "research" is to be based on sources available in the classroom and school library, and on the Web. Unfortunately, the "facts" that students will gather, even from the Web, are inadequate for understanding the Cheyenne's patterns of thinking, their ways of adapting technologies to the bioregion they depended on, their ceremonies and ways of encoding wisdom, their system of communal decision making, and the ways children learned the patterns of the culture. In effect, students are encouraged to project their own cultural patterns onto the Cheyenne they role-play.

A student's imagination is an especially unreliable basis for learning to "see things from others' point of view." Even the use of the Euro-American metaphorical language for naming rivers, territories, and geological formations, rather than the metaphors of the indigenous cultures, further obscures the indigenous ways of experiencing and naming the land—which they did not experience as an empty wilderness waiting to be settled by the European emigrants. The role of metaphor in the simulation is especially interesting, because it brings into question whether students are being given the language of different cultural ways of knowing that would enable them to "see things from the others' point of view." The use of the term *emigrant* is generally interpreted by people who have only the most superficial knowledge of the history of the West as interchangeable with the terms *pioneer* and *settler*. As they simulate the decisions of the emigrants, students unconsciously adopt and reproduce the assumptions that the land not already settled by European emigrants was empty, unclaimed wilderness. By entering the mind-set of the emigrants, students are not only learning bad history, they are also learning to think in a way that has particular relevance today: that they have a moral obligation to impose their view of progress (modernization, economic and technological development, and globalization) on supposedly backward and thus inferior cultural groups. Just as Western technology transformed the supposedly unsettled wilderness, today's even more advanced Western technology must transform the current areas of cultural backwardness. *The Oregon Trail II* encodes the same cultural schemata now used to justify the global culture of cyberspace.

This acclaimed example of educational software can also be criticized from an ecological perspective. One of its most serious limitations is that it reinforces the Western bias of the emigrants toward the local knowledge of indigenous cultures. While the emigrants relied on indigenous guides to provide information about where to cross rivers and mountain ranges, the emigrants ignored or viewed as inferior the cultural means by which indigenous cultures attained self-sufficiency without, in most instances, destroying the environment. As the simulation is designed to reproduce the emigrants' mind-set, which was either indifferent or hostile toward learning the accumulated ecological wisdom of indigenous cultures, it teaches today's students to ignore the complexity and significance of local knowledge of the interdependencies of natural systems.

In effect, *The Oregon Trail II* reinforces an implicit attitude that is unlikely to recognize the economic dependencies and ecological degradation that accompanied the emigrants' efforts to make Western technologies the standard for other cultures—which today's governmental and corporate policies still replicate. Nor are students likely to recognize the thread of continuity between emigrant appropriation of indigenous land and current corporate efforts to patent genetic codes of centuries-old indigenous plants. By placing students in a historical context that presaged today's global economic and technological trends, *The Oregon Trail II* reinforces the assumptions and values that most need to be questioned. In the next chapter we shall consider how the simulation could be modified in ways that would enable students to understand the fundamental differences between the European emigrants and the indigenous cultures and how these differences impacted local ecosystems.

Of the hundreds of educational software programs being purchased by school districts, the Sim series produced by Maxis is especially noteworthy. All the programs place students in decision-making situations where they must consider a wide range of variables in planning and running a city (*SimCity 2000* [1993]), or the Earth's ecosystems (*SimEarth* [1991], *SimLife* [1995], *SimAnt* [1991]). Unlike most educational software, the teacher's manual to *SimEarth* contains an explicit statement about the two assumptions that underlie the simulation: the still unproven Gaia theory of James Lovelock and the assumption that intelligence is an evolutionary advantage. But other culturally specific ways of thinking encoded in *SimEarth* and the other Sim programs are not acknowledged.

Common to all the Sim programs is the assumption that complex systems, such as an ant colony, a city, or the earth itself, can be scientifically managed. Ironically, these supposedly environmentally sensitive programs propagate the most extreme expression of Western hubris: that science and technology can solve all the challenges of Nature. For example, the educational significance of *SimLife* is explained in the following way:

> *SimLife* is the first genetic engineering game available for personal computers. It lets players manipulate the very fabric of existence,

giving life to creatures that defy the wildest imaginations. Players create exotic plants and animals of various shapes, sizes, and temperaments, and turn them loose into a custom-designed environment in which only the best-adapted species survive! With *SimLife*, the budding mad scientist can people the landscape with mutagens (agents that cause mutation and, indirectly, evolution). Or change the individual genetics of one creature and see what effects its offspring have on the long-term survival of its species and on the ecosystem as a whole (p. 1).

This anthropocentric, experimental approach to Nature is also the basis of *SimEarth* which, according to the teacher's manual, can be played in either a game or an experimental mode. When played as a game, students must make decisions about the evolution of different species within a limited energy budget. The experimental mode makes available "unlimited energy to mold *your* plant" (italics added). Students are told that "It's your toy—you make the rules. You don't need a goal if you don't want one." They are also given a list of things to do, such as "prevent a particular species from developing intelligence, manipulate the evolutionary path, and play with the atmosphere and see what happens."

Reinforcing this mind-set in students is important for many reasons. First, *SimEarth* reinforces the eco-management assumption that systems designed by humans are superior to the design processes of Nature. As their primary approach to scientific knowledge and responsible eco-citizenship, students learn to assess ideas in terms of data alone and venture into experimental decision making. This reinforces the assumption that experimental inquiry is the highest expression of intelligence and thus is worthy of globalization. Such a mode of thinking has made important contributions to the quality of human life; it has also contributed to deepening the scope of the ecological crisis. Here are just a few examples that can be attributed to an experimentally oriented mind-set: diverting the rivers that fed the Aral Sea; introducing DDT and other synthetic chemicals into the environment; starting the Green Revolution, which has diminished genetic diversity in many populated regions of the world; and introducing technologies that are changing the carbon cycle and thus contributing to global warming.

However, the scale of these experiments with the variables of natural systems is beyond what scientists can fully anticipate and thus control. While eco-management is becoming more aware of the need to think long-term sustainability, experimenting with the foundations of life, as the Sim series teaches, is still viewed as necessary for achievements on the cutting-edge of science. Witness the experiments that now make possible the cloning of animals and eventually humans.

Second, along with the hubris and assumptions that equate scientifically based change with progress, the Sim series, like all other educational software, ignore other forms of cultural storage and renewal—such as elder knowledge and the need to develop symbolic forms of expression (music, dance, narrative, ceremony) that do not diminish the processes of Nature. Third, the emphasis in the Sim series on making decisions that involve the use of modern technologies leaves students without an understanding of the differences between ecologically appropriate technologies and those that are culturally imperialistic.

The increasing use of computers in the classroom is part of the commodification process that is spreading throughout public schools and universities. Just as major corporations are contracting with educational institutions that allow them to market their products more directly and more visibly (including the display of corporate logos and slogans on school buses, hallways, and uniforms) computers in the classroom are also creating reliance on brand-name computer products.

The problem of learning in cyberspace has even more serious implications that the computer industry, classroom teachers, and university professors fail to recognize. While some critics say that classroom computers should be eliminated entirely until students reach a certain stage of physical and conceptual development, I am afraid that the present trend to increase the educational uses of computers will only continue. Thus, a different set of questions seem especially important to consider. Aside from the ever-increasing cost of our technological dependency, three questions stand out from a long list: (1) How do we educate teachers and educational software programmers to become more conscious of the cultural assumptions and values reinforced in computer-mediated educational experiences? (2) Can the software be designed to clarify how certain cultural assumptions and values undermine the convivial and morally reciprocal patterns that characterize more self-reliant communities? (3) What do students need to understand about the cultural non-neutrality of technology and the difference between imperialistic, environmentally destructive technologies versus those that support local knowledge of environmental possibilities and limits? The following chapters will suggest partial answers to these questions and frame the dialogue that must begin.

# 6 Why Computers Should Not Replace Teachers

Two conferences on the educational uses of computers typify how complex educational, political, and ecological issues are being disregarded in the effort to make the computer as necessary to education as the older tradition of print that it is based upon. The conference, sponsored by the Benjamin Franklin Institute for Global Education and given technical support by Pacific Bell, Netscape Communications Corporation, and a subsidiary of Marshall Industries, was conducted in October 1997 over the Internet. The reach of the conference was truly global. The purpose was to showcase the more than thirty thousand college and university courses offered over the Internet. As John Hibbs, the founder of the institute, put it, the purpose of L.E.A.R.N. Day is to hold a convincing demonstration that "students in Bombay can take courses in Boston." Hibbs further claimed that the Internet conference would demonstrate that the technology is not a "fancy telephone for the privileged, but a powerful truck which can deliver the priceless cargo of higher education anywhere on the planet." The cyberspace showcasing of courses and degree programs started in Guam and followed the twenty-four-hour cycle of the sun with live interactive conversations between educators and participants in Australia, China, Japan, Canada, the United States, Mexico, Brazil, Great Britain, France, Germany, Poland, Turkey, Egypt, Russia, and India. All together, twenty-two countries, representing a wide range of cultures and ecological challenges, were linked together in this effort to market the power of the computer. As one electronic press release put it, L.E.A.R.N. Day was "a symbol that knowledge can be brilliantly transferred from anyplace to anywhere." Behind the self-congratulatory rhetoric was another message: The Internet now enables people in the most remote villages in India, China, and other countries to be consumers of Western-style education—and thus to become integrated into the technologically oriented consumer lifestyle.

The second conference focused on a more typical approach to integrating computers into the professional education of teachers. Sponsored by the Northwest Regional Laboratory and the Northwest Educational Technology Center, the conference attracted teacher educators from across the country. Using a laptop-controlled slide projector that continually put the printed text on the screen out of sync with the verbal presentation and thus drew attention to the malfunctioning technology, the keynote speaker, a dean of a college of education in Washington State, framed the challenge facing teacher educators with a story about a six-year-old girl named Emily. Emily will enter the first grade with a broad familiarity with television, videos, and computers. As the dean emphasized, Emily will have already experienced how electronic technologies give her access to entertainment and information beyond her immediate physical environment. The dean then elaborated on how teachers need to be prepared to respond to Emily's attitude toward life in an electronic environment. The goal, as he put it, is to prepare teachers who can create classroom environments where technology is the core of students' experience and learning is a process of students constructing their own knowledge. After urging the audience to adopt a "fearless attitude" toward preparing teachers to integrate computers into the teaching and learning process, he concluded with the observation that Emily and her friends deserve no less. Aside from the high cost of continually upgrading computers and providing equal access to computers for all students, no other concerns were raised. Nor did anyone in the audience of 150 teacher educators raise questions about the speaker's assumptions and willingness to use the experience of a six-year-old child to justify the direction of educational reform.

The other featured speakers repeated what has become a litany within teacher education circles: the connections between computers and learning; the skills needed in the twenty-first-century workplace; the need to cultivate ways of thinking appropriate to a world of constant change; the dependence of a "knowledge-based society" on computers; and (borrowed from the business community) how computers "distribute" learning "on demand" and "just in time." Like the promotional literature and other educationally oriented conferences of the last twenty or so years, the conference on Integrating Technology into the Teacher Education Curriculum did not address educational issues that surround the cultural mediating characteristics of computers. Nor was there any mention of the connections between the commodification process that computers are helping to globalize and the ecological crisis. Indeed, the myth of technologically based progress was as palpable as both the plenary and break-out sessions were predictable.

In criticizing these two events it is important to keep in mind the insights of the French philosopher Jacques Ellul, who identified the essential characteristics of modern technology. His major study of the differences between traditional and modern technology was published in 1954, with the English translation appearing in 1964 under the title *The Technological Society*. After examining the characteristics of technology in traditional societies—its local nature, its subordinate role in mythopoetically ordered cultures, its incremental and conserving pattern of development, and its emphasis on the skill of the worker rather than the complexity and efficiency of the tool—Ellul turned his attention to the characteristics of modern, Western technology. The common traits, he concluded, include what he termed the "automatism of technical choice" (efficiency rather than other human values determines the selection of technology); "self-augmentation" (technical innovations in one area of society lead to corresponding technological developments in other domains of social life—with technological progress being irreversible); "monism" (older techniques and values that do not contribute to efficient ordering of outcomes are displaced); "technical universalism" (the global integration of technology requires universal education to the mind-set that will not disrupt the efficiency of the technology—thus it subverts other cultural knowledge systems); and the "autonomy of technique" (technological development is no longer limited by moral and political concerns but progresses according to its own value system) (1964, pp. 79–149).

With the 20 percent of the U.S. workforce now working in computer-related industries and earning more than the rest of the entire workforce, Ellul's argument of technological self-determinism has to be qualified to take account of the economic self-interest of a powerful segment of the U.S. population. Scientific and technological elite groups in other countries, such as Canada, Great Britain, France, Germany, Russia, India, China, and Japan, are competing for their share of the global computer market—and in the process demonstrating the validity of Ellul's other insights.

There is another point that critics of educational computing need to keep in mind: sound arguments for the reversal of technological developments carry little public influence after the public has already become dependent on the technology. Two examples come readily to mind. First, Jerry Mander's book *Four Arguments for the Elimination of Television* (1977) provided well-reasoned explanations and compelling evidence pertaining to television's destructive impact on family life, child development, political democracy, and social involvement. The book was widely read, but it did not reverse the growing trend of more televisions per household. Second,

Eugene F. Provenzo Jr.'s well-documented book *Video Kids: Making Sense of Nintendo* (1991), which examined the values reinforced in video games (sexism, violent aggression, and competition), should have caused parents and educators to demand basic changes in the industry. Instead, sales of Nintendo and competitive brands have continued to climb. The inability of other critics to reverse technological trends, especially when the technologies become status symbols (such as gas-guzzling sports utility vehicles), is a sobering reminder that arguments, no matter how well reasoned and documented, have little influence in reversing trends that have powerful support systems behind them.

While it is easy to agree with Ellul's analysis of the dominant technological trends, events occurring since he wrote *The Technological Society* provide optimism that the global spread of technological development, while perhaps irreversible, can be limited. Unlike the early stage of postcolonialism following World War II, when Third World development meant the adoption of Western technological and economic values, today there are non-Western cultural groups resisting modernization. The Chipko movement in India began with village women protesting the cutting of trees and quickly became a broad-based conservation movement that also redefined the meaning of development. In the Mexican state of Chiapas, the Zapatista National Liberation Army has drawn world attention to their efforts to resist Western-style development. Less visible in the Western press but more noteworthy is the Proyecto Andino de Tecnologías Campesinas (the Andean Project for Peasant Technologies), whose mission is to regenerate cultural traditions in the Peruvian Andes. Other groups in Africa, Southeast Asia, and North America are resisting modernization because they recognize that their traditional knowledge and values are more harmonious with the ecological realities of their bioregion than the individualistic, consumer-oriented, and technologically addicted lifestyle of the West.

However, optimism has to be tempered by recent changes intended to accelerate the spread of Western technologies and market values. The recent implementation of the North American Free Trade Agreement (NAFTA) and the World Trade Organization (WTO) were purportedly founded to create greater material prosperity for everyone by eliminating barriers to free trade. But the elimination of tariffs and laws that reflected local needs and communal traditions will reduce material prosperity in many non-Western cultures. NAFTA and the WTO force local producers to compete with international corporations that control more wealth than many countries. As Vandana Shiva and Radha Holla-Bhar (1996) point out, these international efforts at economic deregulation allow the Western system of intellectual property rights to be established over indigenous knowledge of biodiversity that previously was "understood as part of the cultural, spiritual, and biological commons" (p. 146). In addition, these trade agreements undermine labor and environmental standards by encouraging the transfer of production facilities to countries with the lowest wages and weakest laws for protecting the rights of workers. As we can see in the radical changes in agriculture Mexico is being pressured to initiate, subsistence farmers are being forced to export their products to U.S. markets while importing crops such as corn, a cultural staple for millions of Mexicans. Like the global spread of computer-based technologies they depend on, these new international agreements represent another experiment with the relationship between cultures and their supporting ecosystems. The past environmental record of the Industrial Revolution suggests that the digital phase that the entire world is now entering will not reverse the increasing stress on ecosystems. The change from the internal combustion engine to microchips has not been accompanied by changes in the deep cultural assumptions and values used to legitimate the "survival of the fittest" ethos that leads to viewing the world's population as an undeveloped market.

The industrial model's scale of impact on the earth's ecosystems reminds us bluntly that we have no alternative but to attempt, yet again, to reverse the current path of technological development. The following explanation of the cultural reproduction characteristics of computers is an attempt to redirect education so that individuals and communities might regenerate their self-reliance and be less consumer oriented. The many publications, workshops, and conferences intended to explain how to integrate computers into the curriculum fail to address two basic questions: (1) Which aspects of the cultural mediating process do teachers need to be aware of to compensate for computer-induced limitations and distortions in the learning process? (2) How can the study of technology be introduced into the public school and university curricula without fostering the technological mind-set that shapes the path of development in Western and non-Western cultures? This chapter answers the first question: it presents the theoretical framework necessary for understanding why computers should not be viewed as marginalizing the responsibilities of teachers. (From here on the reference to *teacher* is intended to include both public school teachers and university professors.)

## Current Theories of Computer-Mediated Learning and Their Shortcomings

Since computers were first introduced into the classroom, two approaches have been taken to "training" teachers in their use. The first can be found today in the titles of articles in professional journals such as *Educational Leadership* and the *Computing Teacher:* "Providing Teachers with Effective Strategies for Using Technology"; "Integrating Technology into a Preservice Teacher Preparation Program"; and "The Link Between Technology and Authentic Learning." Most of these articles contain lists of procedures, rules to follow, and questions to ask: "insist on interactivity and exploration"; "tap into support services to help with implementation and assessment"; and "navigate the electronic superhighway." These articles provide common-sense suggestions, encouragement to prepare students for the Information Age, and elaborate repetition of previous computer education journal articles. The second approach revives what is interpreted in most colleges of education as Piaget's most profound insight into how children learn. Indeed any reference to the learning process chimes a predictable refrain—"students learn by actively constructing rather than acquiring knowledge"—with only occasional variation. Even Alan C. Kay, Seymour Papert, and Sherry Turkle have made this view of learning the basis of their pro-computer arguments. The popular educational slogan that teachers should be a "guide on the side and not a sage on the stage" represents yet another way of summarizing this view.

Like a mantra, the authority of the statement about student learning lies more in its repetition than in its credibility. Missing is an analysis of the connections between the ecology of language processes that children are embedded in and the acquisition of thinking and metacommunication patterns that enable them to interact with others in their linguistic community. In place of an analysis of the relationship between culture, language, and thought, educators instead rely on the use of god-words that cannot be challenged without appearing to be both reactionary and authoritarian. As Christine Chaille and Lory Britain (1991) put it, one of the most common and problematic extensions of Piaget's constructivist theory of learning is the argument that "as they grow, young children progress from heteronomous dependence upon adults to increasing independence and autonomy. Put simply, *heteronomy* means being subject to external laws and domination, while autonomy is self-government" (p. 8). Rheta DeVries and Lawrence Kohlberg (1990) put it even more succinctly: "Heteronomous relations . . . retard children's development, and autonomous or co-operative relations promote development" (p. 41). The keynote speaker at the conference on integrating computers into teacher education made the same point when be began his presentation by saying that students do not learn by listening. This hubristic statement ignores the major part of human history before the introduction of print, not to mention his expectation that we would all learn by listening to him.

The following statement in the President's Committee of Advisors on Science and Technology Panel on Educational Technology *Report to the President on the Use of Technology to Strengthen K–12 Education in the United States* (1997) suggests how influential the constructivist theory of learning has become: "While the Panel is thus unable to make a confident and definitive statement regarding the superiority of the constructivist approach, it believes there to be a high *likelihood* that many or all of the essential elements of this approach could play a major role in improving the quality of our nation's elementary and secondary schools" (p. 35). The report then concludes that, within the framework of this newer paradigm, technology is viewed not as a tool for improving the efficiency of traditional instructional methods but as one element of a new constructivist approach in which teachers concentrate instead on helping their students to actively construct their own individual knowledge bases and skill sets.

There are many reasons for the widespread embrace of a learning theory that fails to consider the commonsense experience of most adults raising their children within a linguistic community. In addition to the root beliefs of the dominant culture that individuals are increasingly autonomous and change is progressive, another set of related connections helps explain the uncritical acceptance of constructivism by so many quarters of the educational community. The emphasis on the child as the constructor of knowledge appears to support liberal assumptions about freedom, progress, individualism, and an anthropocentric world.

The differences between the three genres of educational liberalism—technocratic, neoromantic, and emancipatory—are over questions of which educational approach will be most effective in achieving the promise of modernity. The approach of technocratic liberals has been to design expert systems (including the use of computers) that foster the individualism needed in a workplace oriented toward material progress in a human-centered world. The emancipatory liberals view the method of critical inquiry as fostering a greater sense of autonomy and, consequently, human-centered progress. The neoromantic educators, assuming that the student is born with an innate capacity to construct knowledge and to choose the right moral values, view their responsibility as protecting the learning process from adult impositions.

All three positions, in tacitly accepting the Industrial Revolution's bias against traditional cultures that value sustainable relationships in both the human community and the greater biosphere, could easily embrace Piaget's theory of genetically determined stages of mental development (and which Lawrence Kohlberg attempted to extrapolate into stages of moral development). The root metaphors shared by the different expressions of educational liberalism marginalize the influence of culture. Indeed, they lead to a view of culture as an authoritarian threat to individual moral and intellectual development. By basing their thinking thusly, liberal educators have failed to recognize that Piaget, the marine biologist turned child psychologist, did not understand how patterns are intergenerationally reproduced by the linguistic processes of a culture. Each of these traditions of educational liberalism were pursuing, well before the acceptance of Piaget's theories, their own approach to constructivism, which is an inherent aspect of the metaphorical foundations of modern liberalism. Technocratic liberals viewed themselves as constructors of new scientific and technological knowledge, while the emancipatory and neoromantic liberals argued whether students' ability to construct their own knowledge is innate or emancipated from the conditioning influence of culture. Ironically, the romanticism implicit in all three forms of educational liberalism has eclipsed the reality that Piaget's theory is based on the same scientific metanarrative that explains the genetic predetermination of every aspect of human and cultural life. This metanarrative explains the symbolic dimensions of thoughts, values, and behaviors as subject to the same laws of adaptation and survival of the fittest that are the basis of Nature's design processes—which are, over the long run, out of our control.

In contrast to the constructivist model, the "cultural transmission model" of education, in which experiential and contextual knowledge is transmitted intergenerationally through face-to-face communication, is regarded by constructivist proponents in the following ways: the "banking" approach to education (Paulo Freire [1971, p. 59]), "unidirectional transmission of isolated facts and skills from teacher to student" (President's Panel on Educational Technology [1997]), and "heteronomous relations that retard children's development" (DeVries and Kohlberg [1990]). The cultural transmission model, in their view, represents the source of miseducation that undermines students' well-being. While admitting that the phrase *cultural transmission model* is both awkward and misleading because it suggests a sender-receiver process of intergenerational learning, it nevertheless foregrounds the primacy and inescapable nature of the cultural milieu.

A better term for the essential relationships that constructivists tend to ignore is the *cultural ecology of intergenerational relationships.* This phrase foregrounds culture as an ecology of relationships that reproduces, renews, and modifies the symbolic legacy of previous generations. As part of everyday experience, these patterns include earlier forms of metaphorical thinking encoded in the spoken and written word, the design of clothing and buildings, the layout of cities—which we initially encounter as an implicit part of the world we are born into. While the constructivists view culturally acquired knowledge as unilaterally oppressive and limiting, a more balanced view might be that in a positive context it cultivates an individual's creative potential, while in a negative context it may thwart development and result in pathologies. The influence of culture may lead to the development of certain potentialities while limiting others. While the outcome is seldom as predictable as the constructivists would have us believe, the "givenness" of the culture that the infant first encounters makes it necessary to use a cultural model to explain both the limitations of the constructivist model of learning (which is used to justify the efficacy of computer mediated learning) and to understand the teacher's role in relation to how computers amplify and marginalize cultural forms of knowledge.

As I wrote this chapter, Great Britain's Prime Minister, Tony Blair, announced that all students in Britain's 32,000 schools will be connected via the Internet to a "national grid for learning" by the year 2002. Germany's Minister for Education and Science recently launched an effort to link up 10,000 secondary schools by the year 2000, while Singapore's government is planning to use computers to create a national system of "thinking schools." The "virtual teacher centre" being established in Great Britain will provide each of the seven million schoolchildren with their own e-mail address (which will likely pressure parents to purchase a home computer). Bill Gates, who is an advisor to British government officials promoting this radical and highly experimental change in education, responded to critics and concerned teachers who questioned the wisdom of the government's plans by reassuring them that "technology is just a tool in the hands of the teacher." The image of the computer as "just a tool" was also central to the thinking of the Panel on Educational Technology when they stated in their report to President Clinton that "students may also use the computer as a tool for various forms of simulations," ranging from problem solving to artistic compositions and designing systems (p. 115). While computers are being promoted as an educational "tool" that empowers students and contributes to national prosperity, they are far more complex and problematic than this image of a neutral tool suggests.

### Computers and Socialization to a Cultural Form of Intelligence

Before addressing the complex set of relationships and processes that come into play in computer-mediated learning, I first would like to address a basic misconception shared by teachers at all levels of the educational process: that intelligence is an individual attribute. This view is the basis of the constructivist position, whether it is expressed in the neoromantic argument that children "construct knowledge through their intellectual activity and make it their own" or in Paulo Freire's equally naive (though politically correct) view that "to speak a true word is to transform the world." The early twentieth-century racist arguments for measuring intelligence through an English language test, and the more recent claims by Richard J. Herrnstein and Charles Murray (1994) that genetic makeup accounts for 60 percent of intelligence, are also based on the misconception that intelligence is an individual attribute. Even Howard Gardner's theory (1983) of seven forms of intelligence is individually centered. Robert J. Sternberg, perhaps the most prolific writer on the nature of intelligence, proposes a "triarchic theory" of human intelligence that attempts to explain, among other things, "the mental mechanisms that underlie intelligent behavior," and the "use of these mental mechanisms in everyday life" (1990, p. 268). The flood of research papers, books, and popular press accounts of the latest findings of brain research reinforce this individually centered view of intelligence. According to scientists, electrical impulses flowing through the billions of neurons in the individual brain account for the various expressions of human intelligence.

If we accept the idea that cognition, creativity, meaning, intuition, and self-identity are all internal states of consciousness totally unique to the individual, we would have to ignore the shared patterns that make communication possible with other members of our linguistic community. In short, we would have to ignore the patterns of daily experience in order to uphold an image of intelligence that goes back to Plato and has been the center of a largely sterile debate among Western philosophers ever since.

Gregory Bateson's explanation of the ecology of mind (1972) provides a view of intelligence that considers how individuals are nested in the symbolic world of culture and how culture is nested in the energy exchanges that characterize local and global ecosystems. His view helps us understand more clearly how earlier forms of cultural intelligence (cultural maps) are encoded and reproduced in the language that we first learn to think in and communicate with.

Bateson's description of intelligence as participatory and inclusive of all the interactions occurring in the larger community of natural systems separates him from Western philosophical and psychological traditions. Two of his statements are especially useful. In *Steps to an Ecology of Mind* (1972) he writes that "in no system which shows mental characteristics can any part have unilateral control over the whole. In other words, *the mental characteristics of the system are immanent, not in some part, but in the system as a whole*" (p. 316). He also addresses directly the error of considering intelligence as an attribute of the autonomous individual: "The total self-corrective unit which processes information, or, as I say 'thinks' and 'acts' and 'decides' is a *system* whose boundaries do not all coincide with the boundaries either of the body or of what is popularly called the 'self' or 'consciousness'; and it is important to notice that there are *mul-*

*tiple* differences between the thinking system and the 'self' as popularly conceived" (p. 319).

The cultural tradition of viewing ourselves as observers who think about and act upon an external world makes it difficult to recognize that Bateson provides a more accurate way of understanding that our environment is coterminous with our relationships. To describe an individual or a plant, in Bateson's way of thinking, one must consider the larger system of which is it a part. To cite a different kind of example, the unit of intelligence in a conversation involves all the participants, including the nonhuman elements that influence the patterns of interaction. In the interactions occurring within a system we find the basic units of information or ideas. Bateson describes this as a "difference which makes a difference." To use his famous example of the individual cutting down a tree with an ax, each swing of the ax causes a change in the surface of the tree. This change is a "difference" or unit of information that leads the individual to change the angle of the next swing of the ax. The information flows in a circuit—or through what Bateson refers to as information pathways. To cite another example, when we engage in a face-to-face conversation, the patterns of metacommunication (changes in tone of voice, pauses, eye contact, physical spaces, facial expression, and so forth) represent the ongoing and reciprocal responses to the "difference which makes a difference." And as every teacher knows, when students are passive or distracted by outside events, efforts to raise the discussion to a higher level of insight and participation seems to falter. But when students are actively involved, the level of intelligence increases for everyone. The expression of intelligence, like conversing or cutting down a tree, is participatory—and is expressed in the response to the differences that arise in the relationship.

Several examples may help clarify his statement that the mental characteristics of the system are immanent in the system as a whole.

The devastating flooding of the Mississippi River that occurred several years ago is now recognized as caused by the cultural mind-set that built the dikes and other navigational systems and located towns in the flood plains. If the "humans-can-engineer-and-thus-control-nature" form of intelligence had not been imposed on that natural system, the "differences" introduced into the system and subsequent ecosystemic behaviors would not have occurred (at least not to the same degree). The system of dams along the Columbia River, which changed the ecosystems along the entire river system and now threatens a number of salmon species with extinction, expresses the immanence of a cultural mind-set that continues to influence the system as a whole, in ways not anticipated by the engineers who designed the dams. To cite a very different example, the Western mythopoetic narrative that provided the moral and conceptual basis of gender discrimination continued to be immanent in the style of architecture, legal system, patterns of discourse, and academic distinctions between high- and low-status forms of knowledge and cultural achievement.

While Bateson understood the unit of intelligence as including all the responses to differences occurring within a system, he recognized that humans do not process information in the same way as other organisms and physical systems. In addition to the physiological level of response, humans make sense of "differences" in terms of the metaphorical patterns of thinking of their cultural group. Bateson recognized that the metaphorical thought patterns of humans, like maps, influenced which aspects of the territory (information exchanges within a system of relationships) would be recognized and how they would be interpreted. Just as the cultural map of patriarchy made it difficult to recognize the potential of women, the cultural map of anthropocentrism (which represents humans as the dominant species and Nature as an economic resource) makes it difficult to recognize that the unit of survival is not humankind but the earth's ecosystems. A cultural map that interprets change as progress eclipses the cultural patterns that are re-enacted over generations as implicit traditions. The power of a cultural map to limit receptivity to environmental messages, such as dying birds and embryos deformed from differences introduced by DDT, needs to be understood in terms of how the maps are intergenerationally passed along and become the basis of the child's conceptual map. Bateson's observation about mental characteristics being immanent in the system can be paraphrased to highlight the immanence of root metaphors in the language and thought processes of a cultural group.

The influence of the mechanistic root metaphor, by contrast, can be seen in Johannes Kepler's statement in the seventeenth century that "my aim is to show that the celestial machine is to be likened not a divine organism but to a clockwork." The immanence of this root metaphor pervades every aspect of modern life: medicine, architecture, education, brain research, the Human Genome Project. Marvin Minsky (1988), one of the early contributors to the field of artificial intelligence, explains consciousness in terms of the "signal-signs (that) steer the engines in our minds." In a widely used educational psychology textbook, Anita Woolfolk (1993) gives the following account of how thought occurs: "Like a computer, the human mind takes in information, performs operations on it to change its form and content, stores information, retrieves it when needed and generates responses to it" (p. 241).

The following summary highlights the difference between the view Bateson presents of our cultural maps and the view of intelligence promoted by the advocates of educational computing: (1) thinking is metaphorical—when seeking to understand the new in terms of the familiar and when utilizing the conceptual schemata encoded and reproduced in everyday language; (2) language reproduces earlier analogues framed by the prevailing root metaphors and thus carries forward earlier expressions of cultural intelligence (cultural maps); (3) when children acquire the vocabulary necessary for spoken discourse and metacommunication, they are learning to think within the earlier expressions of cultural intelligence encoded in the metaphorical constructions of language. While learning these implicit thought patterns, young children may engage in highly imaginative expressions of metaphorical thinking. These new expressions are ephemeral when compared to how quickly their thinking patterns reproduce the cultural schemata of change as progress, humans as the center of nature, and individuals as the source of moral authority and rational choice. The personal pronoun *I* quickly becomes a dominant force in framing relationships.

If we foreground the historical aspects of the cultural ecology encountered by children who are supposedly constructing their own world, we see how philosophers and other theorists over the last four hundred years re-created language to legitimate elite groups promoting the advancement of a scientific, technological, consumer-based culture. We can also see how our current language reinforces this modern conceptual map and carries forward this earlier form of cultural intelligence—which is reproduced in the explanations of how children construct their own ideas and think with data. While young children may recognize analogies that are new to adults, the orthodox metaphorical constructions they encounter through the media, discourse of parents and teachers, and, eventually, university professors will largely displace the knowledge they construct through their own intellectual activity. By the time children begin formal schooling they already take for granted the cultural interpretative framework that represents them as autonomous individuals who make their own choices and that leads them to view change and consumerism as expressions of progress. They have also learned many nonverbal cultural patterns of communication.

We can understand more clearly the teacher's responsibility for supplementing the limitations of computers if we summarize the cultural orientations that the technology promotes and diminishes. While there are widespread discussions about the need to expend huge sums of money on equipping public schools and universities with the latest computer technology, we never hear of the impact of computers on cultures that have not already been overwhelmed by high-status, consumer-oriented knowledge. The mounting evidence of environmental degradation, which has become a prominent feature of media coverage, bespeaks the urgency of considering the impact computers have on the symbolic foundations of the world's cultures.

## Computers and Culture: What Is Promoted, What Is Diminished

Computer-mediated thought and communication promote the following culturally specific patterns: explicit and decontextualized knowledge (data, information, and models, with no clear authorship); subjective judgment and individual autonomy; language as a conduit of sender–receiver communication; subjective experience of temporality, where the value of cultural traditions and responsibility to future generations is individually determined; instrumental and subjective morality; and human–Nature relationships dominated by anthropocentrism.

The cultural patterns diminished by computer-mediated learning include implicit, contextual knowledge; the metaphorical nature of the language and thought process; awareness of the past and future as influences on present-time decision making; moral reciprocity based on mythopoetic narratives and intergenerational face-to-face communication; and awareness of interdependence and the sacredness of Nature.

In some areas of computer use, such as in medicine, engineering, and certain areas of scientific research, these characteristics of computers might not be so critical. But they are important to understanding computer-mediated learning—and the cultural implications of using computers in eco-management. The focus here, however, will be on how computers in educational settings, in reinforcing a Cartesian way of thinking and subjectivity, create a special challenge for teachers.

## Computer-Mediated Learning As Primary Socialization: Responsibility of Teachers

*Primary socialization* is a phrase I have used in previous books to describe the way in which individuals, when learning about a new aspect of cultural experience, initially depend on other people (significant others) who are sharing what they have already learned. In an educational setting, the student is often dependent on the teacher and on the people who write the textbooks, educational software, and other curriculum materials. While students undergo primary socialization in other settings where parents, peers, and the media serve as the significant other, much of their initial understanding of different aspects of cultural life will be mediated through the teacher's tacit and explicit understandings. That is, when students learn something for the first time, they are dependent on significant others for the symbolic frameworks that provide the basis of understanding—which is another way of saying that students learn largely what the language given to them by others enables them to think.

Understanding the areas of dependency and how the teacher mediates the student's encounter with a new area of cultural experience (such as how to think about historical events, technology, competition, data, and so forth) is important for two reasons. First, if teachers understand the language processes that come into play when a student is learning something for the first time, they can make decisions that will facilitate the development of the student's communicative competence. On the other hand, if primary socialization is limited to passing on the teacher's implicit values and thought patterns, students may be left without the symbolic framework necessary for understanding the complexity of what is being learned—and thus be unable to articulate the relevant issues. Second, the influence of teachers (and significant others from various sectors of cultural life) extends beyond the current generation of students. As the students become adults and take on the role of significant other for the next generation, they will reproduce many of the cultural values and patterns of thinking they learned in their earlier dependency relationships.

Just as books, videos, and classroom discussions introduce students to the shared understandings we call "curriculum," computers are also part of this primary socialization. Before clarifying the special challenges that accompany the educational use of computers, I'd like to summarize briefly the key areas of decision making that teachers need to be aware of and the probable educational consequences when teachers adopt the view that "students construct their own knowledge" and when they use the primary socialization patterns of the media, most family and work situations, and the discourse of everyday encounters.

Aside from behaviors that model how to act, dress, and metacommunicate in different social settings, which may involve primary socialization, the linguistic processes mediated by the significant other represent the most influential part of this cultural reproduction process. The key point overlooked by constructivist educators and proponents of educational computing is that the schemata reproduced in the metaphorical constructions of the language are the basis of thought. Data and information are conceptually organized and interpreted in accordance with the metaphorically based schemata learned and reinforced over a long history of primary socialization—which also has biographically distinct elements. For example, economists still organize data in terms of a cultural schema learned in the early grades that excludes housework, and most adults continue to reproduce their English teacher's way of thinking about the use of metaphor. The cultural schemata that equate progress with better engineering and life as secular are understood by scientists who are developing the cloning technology for customized human organs. Other examples of cultural schemata based on the root metaphors of individualism, anthropocentrism, patriarchy, and, for some groups, "original sin" can easily be cited.

If we can avoid thinking of language as a conduit, we can then recognize the linguistic processes that teachers make decisions about when students are in the dependency relationship at the initial stages of primary socialization. If we set aside the nonverbal processes of primary socialization by focusing on how students learn, for example, about the scientific method or the history of the West, we can recognize the specific ways in which the teacher mediates the language acquisition process. When students are learning about some aspect of cultural life for the first time, the first words used to explain attributes and relationships generally become the initial basis of understanding. The use of analogic thinking and iconic metaphors in this initial phase of learning often reproduce the prevailing root metaphors. When the language encodes the same root metaphors that underlie what students have learned elsewhere, learning is easier and less stressful. Unfortunately, neither students nor teachers recognize the problematic nature of what is reinforced.

In addition to making decisions about the language that provides the initial basis of understanding, the teacher makes additional decisions about the language processes that are at the heart of primary socialization. These decisions include ensuring that the language and theoretical framework represent the complexity of the lesson's focus. The teacher's choice of language must consider the student's conceptual and experiential development. When the curriculum corresponds to the teacher's beliefs, and when the teacher lacks an in-depth understanding of the subject, primary socialization too often becomes a matter of acquiring a simplified language and theory framework—one that primarily reproduces the teacher's implicit understanding.

At the same time, the teacher has the responsibility of determining whether the initial language is too abstract and thus unrelated to the students' own cultural background of experience. Providing the language that encourages students to contextualize in terms of their own experience what otherwise might be briefly memorized and categorized as irrelevant requires a teacher's constant attention. At times the cultural background of students may serve to clarify the deep moral and conceptual differences between cultures—such as learning the different views of creativity as individualistic and competitive or communal and cooperative.

Teachers also confront choices about the metaphorical nature of language. These decisions are really about the appropriateness of the cultural framework that is reproduced in the linguistic processes of primary socialization. Whether teachers are aware of it or not, they are making several decisions: about the appropriateness of the analogue to explain new concepts and whether differences are more important than similarities; about the level of attention given to the history of iconic metaphors—what is encoded in such words as *data, intelligence, consumption,* and so forth; about the time to help students recognize that while an analogue provides the initial basis of understanding, it involves an "as if" way of thinking and should not be viewed as representing reality; and lastly, about explaining the culture's root metaphors and how they came into existence, and examining whether they should continue to be the basis of current thinking and values. However, this responsibility should not be interpreted as giving teachers license to use the classroom to promote their own political agenda. Decisions about the linguistic processes that constitute primary socialization are really about which cultural traditions and models of intelligence will be passed along to students, and whether these cultural maps enable students to understand the essential changes occurring in their communal and environmental relationships.

Regardless of whether it involves learning about authors, historical events, methods of problem solving, or current issues and relationships, primary socialization also involves making decisions about when to point out students' assumptions and behavioral patterns. Correspondingly, teachers must be able to recognize the problematic cultural assumptions encoded in the curriculum materials—including educational software. The most difficult challenge for teachers is recognizing their own implicit assumptions. If they are unable to do this, they will not recognize the assumptions encoded in curriculum materials and the students' assumptions that correspond to their own thought patterns and values. A further challenge is knowing when to let certain background assumptions be implicitly reinforced. Advocates of the various approaches to educational emancipation often overlook the fact that pointing out implicit cultural patterns is a politicizing process that may, in turn, lead to reactionary thinking that undermines a consensus achieved over many years of struggle. Asking students to make up their own minds about whether women should have the same rights as men, whether we should have a Constitution and Bill of Rights, and whether we should value cultural and species diversity are examples that point to the need to avoid turning the examination of implicit cultural patterns and beliefs into a formula where students are encouraged to question everything on the assumption that traditions are inherently oppressive.

Teachers need to be aware of another aspect of primary socialization. When students learn something for the first time, and when what they are reading or listening to is represented as objectively real, they often have inadequate background knowledge for recognizing that it has human authorship and thus represents a culturally specific interpretation. At times, their previous patterns of primary socialization may enable them to recognize the misrepresentations. But teachers have an ongoing responsibility for pointing out when important aspects of the culture are being interpreted by students as objectively real. That is, teachers are continually faced with making decisions about whether to put the "facts" or some objectified form of knowledge into a historical and comparative cultural perspective.

Primary socialization in educational settings requires teachers to mediate between past ways of thinking and the current generation's need to revise and, in some instances, reaffirm the past in terms of the ever-changing state of communal and environmental relationships. Unfortunately, few teachers understand the dynamics of this process. They do not understand the cultural mediating processes that are unique to their professional responsibility. It is similar to a doctor who does not understand human anatomy and a lawyer who does not understand the Constitution. This lack of understanding, in part, can be traced to the root metaphors that underlie academic disciplines and teacher education. The root metaphors that represent the individual as autonomous and change as inherently progressive also require that language be viewed as a conduit, otherwise the view of individually centered rational thought would need to be set aside. These assumptions, as stated earlier, put out of focus how the language used in educational software reproduces the conceptual and moral templates of a cultural group. Liberal ideologies, as reflected in the thinking of constructivists and proponents of educational computing who view data as the basis of thinking, also contribute to this professional myopia.

There is a minority of teachers who are sensitive to the miseducation that occurs when the language is abstract, limited, and metaphorically misleading. They also know when to point out the implicit and when to reframe facts and objective knowledge in their historical and cultural contexts. Their own past socialization may have made them aware of the complexity of intergenerational learning. Their deeper understanding of the content is also an important factor. A superficial knowledge of curriculum content inevitably produces a primary socialization based on limited and abstract language, and the use of metaphorical constructions that unknowingly may be misleading. Unfortunately, most classroom teachers, professors of education, and software developers are indifferent to the values and assumptions reinforced in educational software. The current trend of teaching more of the curriculum through computers, and thus further marginalizing the responsibility of teachers, must also be seen as a form of maleficence, which is further compounded by the software developer's profit motive. Developers continually update their educational software to ensure that it is politically correct by including pictures of women and members of minority groups; but they continue to ignore the cultural differences in ways of knowing and how the beliefs reinforced in the software propagate environmental degradation.

We need to reconstitute the deep metaphorical foundations of our modern cultural maps so that we may become more aware of the messages circulating through ecosystems that our cultural practices are not sustainable over the long term. For example, while the increase in the U.S. population will require more productive farmland, the rapid spread of suburbia and the accompanying network of roads are putting out of production over two million farm acres each year. The rapid depletion of aquifers across the country is also part of the ecological information system that largely is being ignored in terms of its cultural implications. The increase in extreme weather systems, which scientists associate with global warming, is yet another aspect of the ecosystem that is not viewed as having a causal link with the cultural practices now being globalized. Unfortunately, most families and participants in work settings are not inclined to examine the dominant culture's conceptual and moral maps, which marginalize the importance of ecological information (except as a problem requiring a technological solution). Nor are many families or work settings likely to encourage an examination of the more self-reliant patterns of traditional and less materially oriented cultures, even though this would help put the patterns of the dominant culture in clearer focus as well as help in the recognition of lifestyles that are more interdependent and community centered. However, it is a possibility in school settings—provided that teachers recognize the extent of the ecological crisis and understand how their mediating role in the process of primary socialization contributes to the students' communicative competence. Teachers also need to avoid being taken in by the myth that computers are simply a complex tool that ensures social progress. Indeed, the complexity of understanding the cultural amplification and reduction characteristics of computers makes the teacher's task even more complicated.

## Changing Computer-Mediated Socialization in the Classroom

The cultural patterns reinforced by computers and the mind-set of educational software developers make it especially important that teachers understand the dynamics of primary socialization. Without an understanding of the way language reproduces past ways of thinking and influences the students' growth in communicative competence, teachers will not recognize the miseducation that educational software promotes. To illustrate, I will use the software programs discussed earlier to show how an understanding of the dynamics of primary socialization can turn even the most ecologically problematic software into a positive learning experience. Of course, it would be better if educational software promoted the lessons of living less materialistic and technologically dependent lives, particularly since few teachers understand their roles as cultural mediators, and even fewer recognize the diverging trends of growing human demand and the viability of Nature's life-giving systems.

As pointed out earlier, the main emphasis in *Storybook Weaver* is to foster students' ability to express their creative imagination in writing. The visual setting of the student's story is created by arbitrarily compiling plants, animals, mountains, oceans, architectural styles, and so forth. As the classroom use of computers is often unsupervised, primary socialization into a value and belief system of complete relativism may occur without the teacher being aware of it. The many variables in a typical classroom make it impossible to discuss all the possibilities for turning this software program into something more than indoctrination into the core assumptions and values of technological materialist society. However, the identification of a few possibilities will help clarify the teacher's responsibility for correcting the miseducation that too often occurs when students interact with the mind-set of the software designers.

In the elementary grades, there are myriad ways that primary socialization can be changed into imaginative yet informed learning. One is to have students write their own stories, read traditional Western folk tales, and then have them listen to an elder whose stories encode the moral insights of her or his cultural group. The ensuing discussion could cover such issues as how the values and assumptions in the students' own stories differ from those of a traditional folk tale and from the oral tradition still anchored in generations of experience within a bioregion. In addition to clarifying the fundamental differences between cultural orientations, there could be a discussion of the students' experience with these three approaches: the private experiences of reading and writing and the participatory experience of oral presentation. The discussion would lay the initial basis both for understanding differences between modern and traditional cultures and for overcoming the bias that favors print-based cultures as superior. There could also be a discussion of the differences between the subjective values of the student and values that represent elder knowledge. This, in turn, could lead to a discussion of the difference between elder knowledge and traditional ways of thinking that are no longer relevant or even destructive. While the vocabulary at this level would not include terms such as *context-free, intergenerational,* and *moral insight,* these concepts could be communicated by using language that is calibrated to the students' background. This more complex and contextually grounded vocabulary, as well as the clarification of the deep cultural assumptions (connected with context-free, subjective, and intergenerational ways of knowing) would substantively change the process of primary socialization.

One of the dominant tendencies of modern consciousness is to disregard the formative influence of context, whether cultural or natural. For example, to question why giraffes and icebergs don't go together would provide the language necessary for observing and thinking about the development of an organism and what constitutes its environment. Students would be acquiring the language that more accurately represents the complexity of Nature and the many facets of the culture–Nature relationship. It would also be a more contextually grounded and more metaphorically sound language. Most importantly, it would help students understand that creative imagination is constructive only when it takes account of how we, as cultural beings, are nested in the natural world.

The educational goals of *DynoPark Tycoon* are listed in the Teacher's Guide under the heading of "Nine Steps to Becoming a Successful Tycoon," which raises the question of whether school districts have well-thought-out criteria for expending public funds on educational software that has little or no educational merit. If students have not already been socialized by playing *Monopoly* or its imitators to equate profit making with winning the game of life, they will learn it from *DynoPark Tycoon*. Given that this software socializes students to commodify entertainment, Nature, and human relationships, the question then becomes, How can a teacher turn *DynoPark Tycoon* into an educationally significant experience?

Briefly, the teacher could use the simulation in business thinking to point out the deep cultural assumptions rooted in *DynoPark Tycoon*. The teacher could follow this by examining the historical transition of economic relationships into their current state of dominance. Enabling students to recognize the noncommodified knowledge and relationships that still exist within the community and the natural world would also be educationally significant. A discussion of the differences between a culture that values a theme park approach to Nature and cultures that are less centered on material and exploitative values would add substantially to the students' education. Examining the environmental impact of a theme park would also help students learn to understand the impact of cultural practices and patterns on natural systems. Each of these suggestions for transforming a deeply problematic educational experience indicates that the teacher's involvement in computer-mediated learning is indispensable.

*Oregon Trail II* represents an example of primary socialization to a past form of cultural intelligence that is remarkably current: bringing civilization to the wilderness and to the "undeveloped" people of the world. Learning about the emigrants' trek to the Oregon Territory by simulating decisions about provisions, river crossings, and every other aspect of life in a wagon train really involves learning to think within the conceptual and moral framework for globalizing Western culture. If a teacher does not share the same assumptions as the program's designers (which is unlikely in most instances), he or she could use the banalities of the program's simulated decisions to examine a series of educationally significant perspectives and traditions. How did the indigenous cultures view the arrival of the emigrants? What are the different cultural assumptions about entitlement to land, political authority, and communal responsibility? What are the achievements of indigenous cultures in political governance and technology (especially agriculture and ecosystem management)? How do the assumptions of the emigrants and political leaders, which led to broken treaties, cultures forced off their homelands, and attempts at forced integration into the dominant culture correspond to current assumptions underlying efforts to globalize Western technological and economic development?

Unless the teacher reframes the process of primary socialization by pointing out the differences in cultural values and ways of knowing, students will be simulating the mind-set of the European emigrants who assumed that their possession of the most violent and disrupting technologies were evidence of their cultural superiority. This assumption, in turn, complements another deeply held assumption currently being given further legitimacy by the scientific metanarrative of evolution: that only the fittest survive in the competitive struggle of life. To recall the observations of Kevin Kelly (1994) and Gregory Stock (1993), as Nature is "out of our control," moral judgment is totally irrelevant.

It should not be surprising to most thoughtful observers that highly acclaimed software programs such as *Storybook Weaver, Oregon Trail II, SimCity 2000,* and *Civilization II* are based on culturally specific assumptions that most students are not likely to recognize on their own. Programs with an environmental orientation, on the other hand, appear to foster a sense of objectivity and the culturally transcendent stance of scientific inquiry. As cultural values do not seem to be involved, common sense tells us that teachers would ensure that students adhered strictly to scientific inquiry and learned the scientific knowledge related to their area of investigation. However, closer examination reveals that there are two types of environmental education software, and that each requires a different kind of teacher involvement beyond the usual science curriculum. Programs such as *GLOBE* and the recommendations in *Environmental Education Toolbox* for using "green" software involve collecting and analyzing data on changes in local ecosystems and communicating the data to students in other parts of the country and to governmental agencies. Programs such as *SimEarth* and *SimLife* represent a different genre in that they have students simulating the judgments that are made in scientifically managing the earth's ecosystems. While the emphasis on scientific thinking suggests that students are not being indoctrinated into an ecologically problematic way of thinking, this is definitely not the case. Indeed, the aura of a science-based approach to environmental education makes it all the more important that teachers understand the culturally biased underpinnings of such an approach.

Environmental education programs that involve students in eco-management simulations raise a different set of issues than programs that facilitate the collection and analysis of environmental data. For example, teachers could first engage students in the full range of decision making made available by the designers of *SimLife*. This could be followed by a discussion of the cultural assumptions that underlie *SimLife*. These assumptions could be put in sharper relief by studying the views of an indigenous culture that has survived over hundreds of years in an environment that allowed for less human misjudgment. The Hopi are a good example of how a culture's mythopoetic metanarratives represent humans and other life forms as part of the same moral and spiritual universe. The Hopi culture also illustrates how understanding life cycles and moral reciprocity defines the nature and limits of technological practices. Another example is the Andean peasant culture in Peru. They have consciously rejected the assumptions underlying the modern world view by regenerating the belief system and technologies that sustained them for the last ten thousand years. Their astonishing knowledge of agriculture (their repertoire of edible plants includes over fifteen hundred varieties of quinoa and thirty-five hundred varieties of potatoes) and their ability to increase their population sustainably cannot be dismissed as irrelevant to Western culture. A key question that emerges from this comparative analysis is whether Western science can provide the moral basis of authority that limits the modern propensity to use environmentally destructive technologies. Can the cultural way of knowing embedded in Western science provide for a dialogue with the sentient beings of Nature (which traditional cultures view as the source of wisdom), or does the reliance on observation and experimentation lead to a management approach to Nature?

The teacher can more effectively demonstrate one of the main learning objectives of *SimLife* by introducing a historical perspective, such as studying what actually happened when foreign plants and animals were introduced into this country earlier in the century. A study of how these plants altered species diversity in a given bioregion would illuminate the dangers of human behavior when it is not based on an understanding of the interdependencies within a local biotic area. For example, a study of the changes that occurred when cheatgrass was introduced in Nevada and Utah and what happened when non-native animals such as red foxes and bullfrogs were introduced into California would enable students to recognize the real rather than imaginary consequences that result from their efforts to manage and politicize the environment. Unfortunately, like *SimCity 2000,* which uses the excitement of a competitive game based on achieving power, money, and symbols of public recognition, *SimLife* will most often be played without the guidance of the teacher. While its designers represent it as teaching about the dynamic characteristics of natural systems, it is really teaching students to adopt an experimental, anthropocentric approach to environmental manipulation.

The data collection and analysis approach that characterizes the *GLOBE* Program and the Environmental Education Toolbox, which are more representative of the approaches being taken in environmental education classes, present a different set of challenges for teachers. *GLOBE* involves students in data collection on the quality of air, water, soil, rain, cloud cover, and so forth in the environment surrounding the school. It also has students communicate their findings via Internet to the National Atmospheric and Oceanic Administration's Forecast Systems Laboratory in Boulder, Colorado. Besides conducting careful measurements and learning the characteristics of local ecosystems, students are also becoming part of a major governmental effort to contribute to a more sustainable environment. Both aspects of this computer-mediated learning experience appear laudable. But there is another dimension to this seemingly down-in-the-trenches approach to environmental education. This is brought out in the list of technology that students will learn to use in the data collection process. According to the teacher's guide to the *Environmental Education Toolbox,* students will learn to use interactive videodiscs, the World Wide Web, palm-sized digital measuring and monitoring tools, portable computers, word processors, video cameras, audio conferencing phones, digital cameras, e-mail, and a fax machine. The justification is that all of these technologies are essential to documenting the students' findings and communicating them to an "electronic pen pal." What is really being taught is the superiority of commodified environmental education and technologically mediated communication with others. In short, what students are learning is that understanding environmental changes depends on sophisticated and expensive technology, and that technology plays an indispensable role in preserving the environment.

Again, whether the cultural assumptions hidden within a seemingly straightforward approach to environmental education are critically examined depends on the teacher's ability to recognize them. If the teacher shares the same assumptions as the designers of the program, primary socialization will appear to be about the changes observed in natural systems—but it will also be shaping the students' assumptions about the indispensable nature of technology. For the teacher who is aware of the multiple cultural messages being communicated to students, the program designers' recommendations can be used to help students recognize that other cultures have developed a very complex knowledge of natural systems that draws from experiential wisdom rather than technology. The data-collection-and-analysis approach to environmental education can be supplemented by the study of how different cultures learn about the environment and use this knowledge to live within its limits.

There is yet another way in which the primary socialization connected with this software needs to be expanded. The emphasis on measuring changes in the environment contributes to a fundamental misconception that too often accompanies the scientific method—which is part of the process of primary socialization that students undergo as they learn to collect and conceptually organize data. As students learn how to use the scientific method, they are learning that they are making "objective" observations. They are learning a mode of inquiry that is supposedly free of cultural influences. They are also learning to view science and technology as the chief means of solving environmental problems. Both the scientific mode of inquiry and the privileged status given to science and technology are not free of cultural influence. Only the involvement of the teacher can help students understand how the dominant cultural epistemology (learned primarily in the universities) influences the categories and explanations of relationships and patterns that are being observed. Similarly, only the teacher's involvement in the process of primary socialization will bring out the connections between cultural beliefs and values and the changes occurring in the local ecosystem. Environmental education classes often identify the industrial source of the toxins found in local streams, but they stop there. They fail to mine the deeper connections: how the cultural tenets of individualism, change as progress, and the environment as a natural resource contribute to the consumerism and profit motives that, in turn, cause the industrial plant to dump toxins in the local streams.

In suggesting that only the teacher's involvement can compensate for the limitations of environmentally oriented software, it must be kept in mind that too many science teachers have been socialized to separate their areas of inquiry from cultural values and conceptually organizing assumptions. Understanding that the use of the scientific method has cultural implications, and that most science teachers involved in environmental education are unable to recognize the nature of this influence, helps to clarify the nature of the double bind we now face. One way out of this double bind would be for universities to make the study of the symbolic foundations of culture an integral part of science education. The other approach would be to introduce a comparative cross-section of culturally based ecological practices into the design of educational software. This would be the easier approach, given the resistance to reform that would be encountered in universities. But then the question arises: where would the designers of environmental software learn to recognize the dangers of separating environmental education from an understanding of the environmental impact of cultural practices and beliefs?

Despite my limited optimism for effecting these changes, my main argument holds: students' encounter with the thought processes and values of educational software designers is too often a source of miseducation. While the miseducation continues to profit the corporations that develop and sell the software to schools, it also reinforces the patterns of an individualistic consumer culture that contributes to the deepening ecological crisis. If readers think this is criticism is too general and thus without foundation, I invite you to examine the cultural values and assumptions promoted in such highly acclaimed educational software as *SimLife, SimCity 2000, Oregon Trail II, Civilization II,* and *Storybook Weaver.* If socially and environmentally aware members of the public examine these and other educational software, they will ask similar questions about why teachers and other school officials ignore their own complicity in this process of miseducation.

# 7 Rethinking Technology: What Educational Institutions Can Do

There is an assumption shared by computer proponents such as Esther Dyson and Nicholas Negroponte, by the decision makers and computer system experts who create the virtual universities and Internet-based classrooms, the business leaders and engineers who are moving goods and services into cyberspace, the people who design educational software, and the parents who pressure school officials to purchase more computers for the classroom. The assumption equates the development of new technologies (particularly computer-based technologies) with progress.

To put this another way, they are addicted to technological innovation in the same way that people become addicted to drugs—and the destructive consequences of this addiction are little understood. Like a drug habit, technological addiction provides an experience of short-lived euphoria, followed by the need to acquire a more powerful fix as soon as possible. In computer-based technologies, the cycle of product innovation and obsolescence is becoming shorter and shorter, which fosters the continual obsession to own the latest innovation. Both addictions lead to the redirecting of economic resources to feed the habit while undermining activities essential to the well-being of individuals and communities. This compulsive behavior is also prevalent in our nation's educational institutions.

This increased dependence on technology represents a highly experimental orientation toward the future. That unanticipated consequences, or even major disruptions in the fabric of human-to-Nature relations, may far outweigh the benefits of the new technologies is seldom recognized. Ironically, this dominant aspect of modern life generally is not viewed as a cultural phenomenon; rather, it is viewed from the perspective of the experts who design and integrate technologies into the existing interlocking systems (which involve both mechanical and social technologies). The public understanding is thus shaped by the way scientists, engineers, and the business community perceive the uses and benefits of technology—which is like having the public understanding of drugs shaped by the addicts themselves. When the public is not being socialized to the perceptions and values of these elite groups, it will tend to fall back on the simplistic thinking they learned in public school and the university: that technology is a neutral tool that can be used according to the values and intent of the user. Ironically, it is the liberal view of the individual that contributes, in part, to maintaining this aspect of this cultural myth, which is such a central feature of public schools and universities. If it were understood that a technology such as the phonetic alphabet amplified a certain form of consciousness and patterns of social relations, it would be hard to maintain the idea that individuals are autonomous agents. In effect, the myth of the autonomous, self-directing individual requires the myth that represents technology as neutral.

The acceptance of this mythic understanding of technology carries with it the increasingly visible dangers of rapid environmental degradation. Indeed, these dangers should be understood in terms of the double binds that now characterize nearly every area of technological development. Generally, these double binds are manifested in the scale of efficiencies and control attained through new technologies that, at the same time, have an adverse impact on the environment. For example, as we are now witnessing in fisheries that previously were considered to be inexhaustible, the new technologies used to exploit various forms of marine life exceed the fishes' ability to reproduce themselves. Technological advances in agriculture and forestry have led to similar negative impacts on aquifers, topsoil, and species diversity. The rapid reduction in the size and number of trees now processed in sawmills demonstrate the technological capacity to cut down hundreds of years of growth in minutes. Technological advances in transportation lead to more toxic chemicals being released into the environment. To cite a specific example, the introduction of cars into China's major cities is contributing to an alarming rise in the amount of lead that children are ingesting— a substance that has a particularly disruptive effect on child development. Even the many efficiencies and conveniences of computers cannot escape the double bind that brings into question whether this technology, on the whole, should be viewed as beneficial to humans and the environment. The double bind can be found in the loss of local knowledge and traditions, the undermining of subsistence economies, the further disruption of intergenerational communication and elder knowledge, the loss of noncommodified relationships and activities, the further diminishing of privacy, and the loss of in-depth knowledge informed by experience anchored in a long-term relationship with the environment.

Before the population explosion of the twentieth century and the rise of worldwide consumerism, the double binds were hardly visible. Rather, the myth of progress seemed an attainable reality for many people who felt their lives limited by community traditions and restrictive governments. But the scale of human demands on the environment, including the power of technology to produce a vast array of consumer goods, has radically changed. As a result, natural systems are being exploited and chemically changed to the point where there is less margin for human error. We can no longer introduce cultural experiments into an environment that can now barely support basic human needs for adequate food, shelter, and meaningful work. One consequence of these cultural experiments, such as the increased reliance on technologies that contribute to global warming, is that changes in natural systems are occurring on a scale that new technologies cannot reverse—at least in the time frame that is meaningful for humans. There is a growing awareness within certain sectors of society that technologies must be more carefully assessed in terms of their environmental impact. For example, physicians are being warned about the dangers connected with excessive prescription of antibiotics, and a few corporations are adopting recycling technologies that put fewer toxins in the environment. But this growing sense of caution has not fundamentally altered the technologies that are changing the symbolic systems of cultures that, until now, have not been centered on consumerism. In effect, the growing sense of caution, and even gains in ecologically sensitive technologies, have not eliminated the basic double bind that accompanies the spread of Western technologies, especially computer-based technologies.

We now need to take a radically different approach to technology. An in-depth assessment by the public should occur before experts introduce the technology rather than after it has been integrated into an interlocking system that the public becomes dependent on. There will always be a level of expert knowledge that will initially be more specialized; nevertheless, the public needs to become sufficiently educated about the broad cultural and environmental issues surrounding a new technology if this most fundamental source of cultural change is to be part of the democratic process. Making technology a central focus of the democratic process is very different from our current situation, where too often the scope of political decision making is limited to governmental groups making decisions about funding—largely in response to political pressure and economic inducements by those who are promoting a particular technology. For the general public, the scope of political decision making is mostly reduced to the economic realm, where the principal question is when to purchase the new technology (that is, when to upgrade to the digital camera, television, and so forth).

The suggestion that the public should become informed about the short- and long-term consequences of new technologies will not be welcomed by the elite groups working to develop these technologies. We have a long tradition in the West, particularly within universities, where technological development has taken on a nearly sacred status, of searching for the new without raising questions about the long-term consequences. Indeed, a history of the quest for new knowledge, although framed in terms of a higher moral pursuit of contributing to the further well-being of humankind, will reveal that it provided the new technologies essential to the development and spread of the Industrial Revolution. The need for an informed public debate is even more urgent because of recent technological developments that make it possible for scientists to create genetic duplicates of animals, grow new organs from cloned cells, and insert genes into plants that eliminate their ability to reproduce themselves.

Following the widespread public concern that the technology used to create a genetic duplicate of a six-year-old sheep would be used to clone humans, Edward Berger (1997), professor of biological science at Dartmouth College, published an article in the *Chronicle of Higher Education* urging scientists to convene a conference to clarify how the scientific community understands the scientific and moral issues raised by this development in cloning technology. Berger was emphatic about the need for scientists to retain control of the upcoming debate. "If we scientists do not initiate a detailed public discussion of the important issues," he warned, "we may find that the integrity and freedom of our research enterprise have been taken away from us by politicians and the conservative and religious forces that now so dominate the political and social atmosphere in the United States" (p. A44). A similar argument would have been made if the research leading to the development of DDT (which earned its inventor, Paul Muller, a Nobel Prize) and CFCs had received similar media exposure. As acknowledged earlier, there will always be a gulf that separates the depth of expert knowledge, which is often quite narrow, from public understanding—which is more oriented toward issues outside the scientists' area of interest and competency. There will also be fundamental differences within the public over economic, political, moral, and religious perspectives. Differences in cultural ways of knowing, as well as varying degrees of awareness of environmental issues, will also be an inevitable aspect of public debates about whether public resources should be made available to groups pursuing new forms of knowledge and technology. With the new interpretation by the courts that allows the patenting of living material, the scientists' search for knowledge that leads to new technologies increasingly is being motivated by economic self-interest.

Given the reduced ecological margin for human error, the general public must replace the current assumption that equates technological innovation with progress with an assumption that any new form of technology may bring unintended ecological and cultural problems. Instead of blind optimism toward technological change, we need to take a more cautious, even skeptical view. We also need to challenge our assumptions that limit consideration of how technological waste can be reintegrated into the food web of the environment rather than left as pollution, and of how new technologies can be used to strengthen rather than disrupt the patterns of interdependence within communities. If the public has a broad understanding that technologically based experiments with the moral and conceptual foundations of a culture often have consequences that go beyond economic considerations, they are likely to ask for a more complex form of accountability of the elite groups before they agree to the release of public funds or to grant the licenses necessary for using public space and other resources. This basic understanding of the non-neutrality of technology will lead to an awareness that groups representing the broader interests of society need to move more quickly in acquiring the expert knowledge necessary for challenging the litany of optimistic predictions that accompany the introduction of a new technology.

Although everyday life for most people in modern society is highly dependent on a web of interlocking technologies, there are few social settings where it is possible to learn about their cultural mediating characteristics. There are even fewer settings where people can learn about the principles of ecological design. While computer proponents proclaim the emergence of a new postindustrial era, the daily patterns of existence are mediated by technologies that embody the same deep cultural assumptions that guided the development of the Industrial Revolution. These earlier assumptions about technology have become institutionalized in the Western approach to formal education. Public schools and universities, rather than the home, church, or workplace, are the logical places to learn about the connections between cultures, technologies, and local ecosystems. Unfortunately, few public school teachers or university professors have given serious thought to the cultural mediating characteristics of technology, and even fewer have studied them systematically. The double bind can be simply stated: the one place in society where it might be possible to learn about the cultural nature of technology, other than how to promote its further development, is unable to challenge the myth that equates technological development with social progress. Indeed, public schools and universities are the chief promoters of the myth.

### Education and Technology: An Overview

The reasons for this double bind are complex, but there is a thread of continuity running throughout the history of high-status ideas in the West that explains why the most dominant aspect of modern life is so little studied as a cultural phenomenon. The thread of continuity that connects the myopia of the present with the deep cultural assumptions of the past can be found in the distinction the ancient Greeks made between *techne* and knowledge of the forms or ideas that were free of practical and embodied expression. What the ancient Greeks understood as *techne*, which we now call technology, was seen as a lower order of human activity—thus less important than philosophy (abstract theory) and an inappropriate concern of the educated person. The bias against the serious study of technology has been further sustained by the early Western mind-body dualism, and the history of social class distinctions that encoded the hierarchy articulated by the ancient Greeks and that is still perpetuated by institutions of higher learning.

While Western cultural development depended on a wide range of technologies, the early universities quickly shed their focus on passing on the technical and procedural knowledge that was the basis of law, medicine, and theology. As universities became centers of liberal studies, the acquisition of technological knowledge became the responsibility of the low-status institutes of technology—and, until recently, what were known as junior colleges. Modern universities now increasingly promote areas of study that lead to the development of new technologies—as an outgrowth of science and as a central focus of schools of business and education, departments of psychology, and so forth.

Thus, the bias inherited from the ancient Greeks has continued to be a dominant characteristic of all levels of formal education—but now there is an important difference. While the direct study of the moral and cultural mediating characteristics of technology continues to be viewed as unworthy of inclusion in a liberal education, the promotion of research leading to the development of new technologies has become the primary focus of most professors and university administrators.

Given the complicity of public schools and universities in promoting the myth that new technologies will provide solutions to the increasingly complex and daunting problems faced by the world's cultures, the suggestion that they provide the best hope for democratizing decisions about technology development and use is likely to appear as naive. In *The Culture of Denial* (Bowers, 1997) I argued that universities, and by extension public schools, are unlikely to examine at a deep cultural level how they contribute to the globalization of the technological form of culture that is now commodifying and genetically redesigning the most basic levels of the natural world. As the various groups that make up the environmental movement document the dangers connected with the present economic and technological course we are on, and clarify the connections between the high-status forms of knowledge and the ecological crisis, the critical attitude fostered in universities must shift toward an examination of technology itself. The feminist movement has demonstrated that professors and university administrators, while unable to recognize on their own how patriarchy influenced curriculum development, hiring practices, reward systems, and even patterns of discourse in the classroom, were nevertheless capable of changing previously taken-for-granted patterns of thinking. It was a surprisingly slow process for an institution that prides itself on its superior powers of critical reflection, but it still represents a capacity for change. However, because of the rapid changes occurring in natural systems, there is likely to be less time to make the necessary adjustment in what students are taught about technology. We certainly cannot wait the centuries that it took professors to become aware of the mythic foundations of patriarchy.

This lack of understanding about technology cannot be attributed to a lack of scholarly writing in this area. The writings of Jacques Ellul (1964), Lewis Mumford (1934, 1967, 1970), Langdon Winner (1986), Don Idhe (1979), David F. Noble (1998), Theodore Roszak (1994), Richard Sclove (1995), and Alan Drengson (1995), to cite just a few of the scholars who have studied different aspects of modern technology, represent only a small part of the literature. Unfortunately, few universities offer courses that introduce students to this important body of literature and to the questions about the future direction of modern technology that most need to be examined. The concern about the nature of modern technology will soon have to move from the margins of academia to a more central place in student education. If the university does not provide for an in-depth understanding of these basic relationships, there will be little chance of it being promoted in the public schools.

## Rethinking Technology

Newspaper articles on technology (especially computers) serve as the best evidence of the failure of universities. These articles seldom provide more than the most superficial understanding of issues that should be at the center of democratic debate. It would be more accurate to say that their usual treatment of computers demonstrates an inability to separate the computer industry–generated myths from the realities of the classroom and workplace. The complicity of universities and the print media in leaving the public unprepared to address the cultural non-neutrality of technology has another effect that works against the democratic process. The dumbing-down process, which various elite groups view as a necessary part of the business of promoting new products, makes it even more difficult for citizen groups that make the effort to inform themselves about the ecological and community impact of different forms of technology to influence the direction of public policy.

All citizens should understand the following aspects of technology and thus study them as a required part of university education:

1. *There are differences between technologies developed in Western cultures and traditional, more ecologically centered cultures.* Understand-

ing how the mythopoetic narratives, viewed cross-culturally, influence the direction of technological development is especially important. This should include understanding how changes in the dominant mythopoetic narratives in the West led to changes in approaches to technology, and how the introduction of modern technology undermined the noncommodified traditions of community life.

2. *Democratizing decisions about technology depends on understanding alternative assumptions that influence the dominant approaches to technology.* If the educational process fails to introduce students to alternative ways of thinking about technology, technological decisions will continue to be framed by the same cultural assumptions that gave moral and conceptual direction to the Industrial Revolution—which does not provide a good model of the democratic process or of ecological citizenship. Students should be introduced to the principles of ecological design that are now more widely understood and even applied in modern contexts. Many cultures have learned these principles through careful observation of Nature's design processes in their local bioregion, and they further refined this understanding through intergenerational communication. Students with a modern mind-set, on the other hand, must unlearn their dependence on decontextualized approaches to technology that are based on design principles derived from a machine-based way of thinking. Learning how to relate ecological design principles—solutions grow from place; ecological accounting informs design; design with nature; everyone is a designer; and make nature visible (Van Der Ryn and Cowen, 1996, pp. 54–56)—to different problem-solving situations and contexts should be a required part of the university curriculum (which might then lead to this form of learning filtering down to the public school classrooms). A deep conceptual and practical understanding of these principles is also essential to recognizing when a modern technology may degrade the environment and undermine the interdependence of community life. Ecological approaches to design must have as their goal the reuse of materials into a new industrial cycle or reabsorption into natural systems. That is, technologies need to be designed in ways that mimic

natural systems that do not produce useless and toxic waste. If students do not understand alternative design principles, the political process will continue to be driven by the technological determinism that Ellul identified as a key feature of modern technology—and universities will continue to be the chief promoters of the high-status technologies that have proven so environmentally destructive.

3. *We need a systematic examination of how modern technology contributes to the culturally transforming process of commodifying knowledge and relationships.* Different groups in the environmental movement have recognized the role modern technology plays in a consumer-based lifestyle and the impact this has on the environment. But it is not generally understood in Western cultures, nor is it understood by the elite class in Third World countries who are attempting to use the Western model as the basis of development. The continual quest to turn knowledge, relationships, moral responsibilities, and Nature itself into commodities produced by international corporations is increasingly viewed as the expression of "progress." What needs to be studied as part of formal education (which itself is becoming increasingly commodified) is how different forms of technology contribute to the commodification of what previously represented personal, family, and community-based knowledge and skill. Understanding the long-term consequences of extending market principles into every area of cultural life, and into cultures that previously chose nontechnological forms of development, also requires that students learn about noncommodified aspects of community. Learning about what is now called voluntary simplicity and the networks of mutual responsibility that still exist within different cultural groups may contribute more to prospects of future generations than what is learned in most areas of the university curriculum.

4. *Modern technology requires a more complex view of tradition.* Unlike technologies in traditional cultures, modern technologies embody modern assumptions about change, context-free knowledge, anthropocentrism, and a secular view of Nature. Their design, use, and replacement assume that every form of technological innovation is superior to the traditions that are displaced. In the words of Edward Shils

(1981), modern technology is an expression of the "antitradition tradition" at the core of modern consciousness. The democratic process requires that citizens understand the relationship between technologies and the cultural traditions of everyday life. This, in turn, requires a more complex understanding of the nature of tradition than is provided in most educational settings. Traditions, in effect, are a form of intergenerational intelligence and communication. Earlier forms of cultural intelligence do not always meet today's moral standards, or represent lifestyles that we would find meaningful or even possible. But there are forms of cultural intelligence that continue to be viable, even essential to everyday life — many of which provide for genuine individual and community well-being. The study of the relationship between technology and cultural traditions should include the following: the nature and importance of elder knowledge; the shift from intergenerational communication to expert knowledge and its effect on self-sufficiency and mutual support; and the commodification of traditions and its effects on wealth and poverty.

5. *Technology has an impact on language and patterns of thinking.* In earlier chapters I gave examples of how machines are used as the analogues for understanding life processes such as thinking and genetic reproduction, and even the design aspects of material culture. Moravec (1988) and Kelly (1994) make no distinction between machines (particularly computers) and human life — thus, in their view, the replacement of humans by computers is an inevitable outcome of Nature's design principles. Students need to examine aspects of cultural life that are influenced by the language and thought patterns derived from machines. Furthermore, they need to consider how this language influences moral values and the ability to recognize differences in cultural ways of knowing — including the influence that mechanistic metaphors have on our views of globalizing consumer culture. The connections between technologically driven language and our understanding of human-to-Nature relationships should be considered.

6. *Social justice issues arise from the influence of modern technology on the nature of work.* Technologies such as computers make it possible to

export jobs to regions of the world where unprotected worker rights and low wages have a major impact on the economic viability of families and communities. While this process also disrupts the economic basis of communities in North America, modern technologies continue to be represented in our educational institutions and in the media as embodying our highest forms of knowledge. There are other double binds in our approach to technology that are equally problematic and that our educational institutions continue to ignore. How modern technologies de-skill and progressively replace workers is a trend that needs to be part of the systematic study of technology. Similarly, how different forms of technology influence the distribution of wealth and power in society needs to be recognized if a democratic polity is to be revitalized. The connections between the nature of modern technology, the assumptions that influence how it is used, and the need to expand consumer markets also need to be considered. As knowledge and reciprocal relationships of community life are increasingly commodified there is a growing need for all family members to work in order to purchase the goods and services previously acquired through mutual exchanges. This increase in consumerism, in turn, leads to more energy and resources being converted to consumption and to more waste materials returned to the environment. The dynamics of the modern commodification process needs to be contrasted with cultures that have retained values and relationships that are not mediated by modern technologies and market transactions. In short, students need to recognize how different cultures have retained a balance between work, noncommodified relationships and activities, and the values that have influenced their ability to keep technology more in balance with the needs of the community rather than the needs of the market.

7. *It is important to acquire knowledge about how the cultural mediating characteristics of computers threaten cultural diversity and ecological sustainability.* This should be understood by every responsible citizen, regardless of the culture of origin. The displacement of local knowledge by data, intergenerational communication by arbitrary subjective decision making, and face-to-face relationships by electronic communities

should be a focus of democratic decision making. Similarly, the substitution of computer-mediated learning for human teachers, with their potential for imparting cultural nuances, should also be a central concern in a democratic polity. In addition to contributing to a more rigorous level of public discourse about the influence of computers in the classroom and workplace, as well as on our civil liberties, understanding the cultural amplification and reduction characteristics of computers is essential background knowledge for people who create educational software. Indeed, the "greening" of educational software is absolutely dependent on understanding how earlier forms of cultural intelligence are encoded in the language students encounter on the computer screen. The minds that students encounter as they interact with the software, to restate Roszak's insight, have a formative influence—especially when they are reinforcing patterns of thought that students already learned to take for granted. People who create educational software, as well as expert systems used in other areas of social life, need to understand that the simulations, facts, data, and decision-making frameworks are expressions of a particular cultural way of thinking. Journalists writing about the influence of computers also need to understand the cultural gains and losses connected with their use in different social contexts. Since public schools and universities fail to address technological issues in any systematic and culturally grounded way, journalists take on the role of educators by framing the issues for the public. Too often they contribute to the further dumbing-down of the public in one of the most critical areas of social life.

With more universities undergoing reforms that will make them more responsive to the "forces of the marketplace," and state departments of education using the myth of "worker needs" in the next century as the basis of reforms in public education, there is little ground for optimism that this critical perspective on computers will be taken seriously. Nor is there a real basis of optimism that the above suggestion for curriculum reform will be discussed by educators. When viewed from a historical perspective, we can see that challenges to current orthodoxies have seldom been taken seriously by those in power—until the reform-oriented minority identifies the moral principle that serves as leverage for adjusting to a new set of relationships and priorities. The American Revolution started as a marginalized form of resistance to the existing orthodoxies. The same holds true for the recent antiwar and feminist movements. These challenges to existing power structures and their supporting mythic cultural narratives succeeded in awakening a deeper, less conscious sense of what constitutes essential relationships in life. In the past, concerns about representative government, peace, and equality served as the moral leverage for transforming existing orthodoxies and the elites that perpetuated them. The growing awareness that Nature is responding to the impact of modern technology by reducing the support systems on which our lives depend perhaps will serve as the moral leverage for a new set of educational and technological priorities.

Translating this awareness into curriculum reform will be an especially daunting challenge. Ideological differences that are becoming more visible between and within academic departments represent just one of the many barriers that reformers will face. Even among the small segment of the academic community that studies the impact of science and technology on society, there is disagreement over whether to take a scholarly or activist approach—with the latter being closely linked to efforts to address issues of ecological justice. But the main impediment to making one of the most dominant forces in modern life the focus of systematic and critical study is the myth that, while the use of technology always reflects the outcome of a political process, the technology itself is politically neutral.

Langdon Winner (1986) and others argue that technology is inherently political. For example, the steam engine that could power many other machines transformed the nature of work, led to the commodification of time, and made intergenerationally based craft knowledge irrelevant—to cite just a few of the radical changes it introduced. Closer to home, as Winner points out, the mechanical tomato picker in California led to a reduction in the number of growers from approximately four thousand in the 1960s to six hundred in the 1970s. Overall, the tomato industry witnessed a decline of thirty-two thousand jobs. These and thousands of other examples bring out how the nature of a technology alters social relationships and traditions, changes the basis of self-identity and guiding values, and benefits specific groups while undermining the well-being of others. What makes technology (both social and mechanical) inherently political is that it embodies the thought process and values of the people who designed it—which means the technology embodies the form of cultural intelligence that the designers have acquired in learning the language of their cultural group.

The different aspects of technology I suggested as areas of study (differences between traditional and modern technologies, cultural assumptions that influence the technological direction, the parallel growth of modern technologies and commodification processes and so forth) are also inherently political. Using Michel Foucault's way of putting it (1983), the action of the technology on the actions of other people and other technologies represents the exercise of power. The changes introduced by the technology are thus political in nature. There are gains, losses, and transformations that reflect differences in perspectives and traditions. The introduction of print technology, for example, led to a new network of power relationships displacing older networks—even to the point of changing the patterns of awareness and social interaction. The amplification and reduction characteristics of computers discussed in previous chapters also involve the exercise of power and thus are political.

The recognition of technology's political nature, both in its design characteristics and in its impact on the complex ecologies of human relationships and practices, should lead to broadening how the political education of the public is understood. The recommendations for curriculum reform at both the public school and university level are thus intended to put a more complex understanding of the cultural transforming characteristics of technology (especially computers) on equal footing with other areas of political education—many of which are equally ignored by our educational institutions.

There are a number of groups, such as the International Forum on Globalization and the Loka Institute, that are attempting to raise the level of citizen participation in deciding issues of technology, communities, and the environment. The Loka Institute, for example, is promoting the Danish approach to establishing citizen panels that provide an opportunity for the public to question experts about possible dangers associated with a new technology. The institute is also promoting an understanding of the differences between democratic technologies and those that contribute to the centralization of power and the loss of local knowledge. One of the recent successes of the institute's effort to promote community-based research, as reported in a 1999 "Net Alert," was in getting symposium participants at the American Academy for the Advancement of Science to support a resolution declaring that "decisions on scientific and technical issues should incorporate input from affected communities and other members of the public, as many European nations have done."

The teach-ins held by the International Forum on Globalization and the efforts of the Loka Institute strengthen the networking among other groups working to regenerate democratic decision making at the local level. But it is doubtful whether their efforts succeed in reaching beyond the small segment of the population already informed about the globalization of Western technologies and economic policies. Nevertheless, this is an important segment to reach, as their commitment to eco-justice issues and level of communicative competence helps to identify the important policy issues—which sometimes even get reported in the media.

Given the rate and scale of technological innovation that is putting the world's cultures on an highly experimental and risky pathway of development, there is an especially urgent need to educate a larger segment of the public in ways that will enable it to recognize how present and future lives will be affected by new technologies. The institutions that reach the larger segment of the population and have the potential to counter the dumbing-down process of the corporate-controlled media, are the public schools and universities. Faculty of these institutions need to recognize both the special opportunity and responsibility they have for providing the background knowledge necessary to democratize technological decisions. They also need to recognize that if they continue to ignore the more complex and subtle linkages between technology and hierarchical systems of increasingly centralized political control, they will themselves be transformed in ways that further marginalize forms of education that do not contribute directly to economic growth. Corporations are already acting on the premise that the nation's educational systems represent a huge market for computer-related technologies and brand marketing campaigns (witness the growing visibility of corporate logos in public schools and universities). As corporations further exploit this market, they will change the educational process in ways that will further undermine the potential of democratic decision making to reverse the trend toward globalization and its corresponding ecological consequences.

# References

Abram, David. 1996. *The Spell of the Sensuous: Perception and Language in a More-Than-Human World.* New York: Pantheon.

Alexander, Richard D. 1987. *The Biology of Moral Systems.* New York: Aldine De Gruyter.

Anderson, Edgar. 1967. *Plants, Man, and Life.* Berkeley: University of California Press.

Apffel-Marglin, Frédérique, ed. 1998. *The Spirit of Regeneration: Andean Culture Confronting Western Notions of Development.* London: Zed.

Basso, Keith H. 1996. *Wisdom Sits in Places: Landscape and Language Among the Western Apache.* Albuquerque: University of New Mexico Press.

Bateson, Gregory. 1972. *Steps to an Ecology of Mind.* New York: Ballantine.

Benedikt, Michael, ed. 1992. *Cyberspace: First Steps.* Cambridge, Mass.: MIT Press.

Berger, Edward. 1997. "Scientists Must Convene, Now, on the Ethics of Cloning." *Chronicle of Higher Education* (18 July).

Berger, John. 1979. *Pig Earth.* New York: Pantheon.

Berthoud, Gerald. 1992. "Market." Pp. 70–87 in *The Development Dictionary: A Guide to Knowledge as Power*, ed. Wolfgang Sachs. London: Zed.

Bigelow, Bill. 1995. "On the Road to Cultural Bias: A Critique of 'The Oregon Trail' CD-ROM." *Rethinking Schools* (Fall): 14–18.

Bowers, C. A. 1988. *The Cultural Dimensions of Educational Computing: Understanding the Non-Neutrality of Technology.* New York: Teachers College Press.

———. 1995. *Educating for an Ecologically Sustainable Culture: Rethinking Moral Education, Creativity, Intelligence and Other Modern Orthodoxies.* Albany: State University of New York Press.

———. 1997. *The Culture of Denial: Why the Environmental Movement Needs a Strategy for Reforming Universities and Public Schools.* Albany: State University of New York Press.

Bugliarello, George. 1990. "Hyperintelligence: Humankind's Next Evolutionary Step." Pp. 25–38 in *Rethinking the Curriculum: Toward an Integrated Interdisciplinary College Education,* eds. Mary E. Clark and Sandra A. Wawrytko. New York: Greenwood Press.

Cajete, Gregory. 1994. *Look to the Mountain: An Ecology of Indigenous Education.* Durango, Colo.: Kivaki Press.

Chaille, Christine, and Lory Britain. 1991. *The Young Child as Scientist: A Constructivist Approach to Early Childhood Science Education.* New York: HarperCollins.

Clark, Mary E. "Human Nature—Revised!" Cottage Grove, Oreg.: unpublished manuscript.

Colborn, Theo, Dianne Dumanoski, and John Peterson Myers. 1996. *Our Stolen Future: Are We Threatening Our Fertility, Intelligence, and Survival? A Scientific Detective Story.* New York: Dutton.

Crick, Francis. 1994. *The Astonishing Hypothesis: The Scientific Search for the Soul.* New York: Charles Scribner's Sons.

Cummins, Jim, and Dennis Sayers. 1997. *Brave New Schools: Challenging Cultural Illiteracy Through Global Learning Networks.* New York: St. Martin's Press.

Darwin, Charles. [1859] 1979. *On the Origin of Species.* New York: Hill and Wang.

de Pommereau, Isabelle. 1997. "Computers Give Children the Key to Learning." *Christian Science Monitor* (April 21): 11.

De Vries, Rheta, and Lawrence Kohlberg. 1990. *Constructivist Early Education: Overview and Comparison with Other Programs.* Washington, D.C.: National Association for the Education of Young Children.

*DynoPark Tycoon.* 1994. Minneapolis, Minn.: MECC.

Drengson, Alan. 1995. *The Practice of Technology.* Albany: State University of New York Press.

Dreyfus, Hubert L., and Stuart E. Dreyfus. 1986. *Mind over Machine: The Power of Human Intuition and Expertise in the Era of the Computer.* New York: The Free Press.

Ellison, Larry. 1994. "Foreword." Pp. 4–5 in *The Computer's Guide to the Information Highway.* Redwood Shores, Calif.: Oracle Corporation.

Ellul, Jacques. 1964. *The Technological Society.* New York: Alfred A. Knopf.

Esteva, Gustavo. 1996. "The Revolution of the New Commons." Oaxaca, Mexico: unpublished manuscript.

Evenson, Laura. 1997. "Computers in the Lives of Our Children." *San Francisco Chronicle* (February 2): 3.3.

Feyerabend, Paul. 1975. *Against Method: Outline of an Anarchistic Theory of Knowledge.* London: Verso.

Foucault, Michel. 1982. "The Subject and the Power." Pp. 208–226 in *Michel Foucault: Beyond Structuralism and Hermeneutics,* eds. Hubert L. Dreyfus and Paul Rabinow. Chicago: University of Chicago Press.

Freire, Paulo. 1971. *Pedagogy of the Oppressed.* New York: Herder and Herder.

Gardner, Howard. 1983. *Frames of Mind.* New York: Basic Books.

Gates, Bill. 1995. *The Road Ahead.* New York: Viking.

Geertz, Clifford. 1973. *The Interpretation of Cultures.* New York: Basic Books.

Gibson, William. 1984. *Neuromancer.* New York: Ace.

GLOBE Program. 1995. *Global Learning and Observation to Benefit the Environment.* Washington, D.C.

Goodenough, Ward H. 1981. *Culture, Language, and Society.* Menlo Park, Calif.: Benjamin/Cummings.

Gross, Paul R., and Norman Levitt. 1994. *Higher Superstition: The Academic*

*Left and Its Quarrels with Science.* Baltimore: The Johns Hopkins University Press.

Hall, Edward. 1977. *Beyond Culture.* Garden City, N.Y.: Anchor.

Harding, Sandra. 1998. *Is Science Multicultural? Postcolonial, Feminism, and Epistemologies.* Bloomington: Indiana University Press.

Havelock, Eric. 1986. *The Muse Learns to Write: Reflections on Orality and Literacy from Antiquity to the Present.* New Haven, Conn.: Yale University Press.

Heidegger, Martin. 1962. *Being and Time.* New York: Harper and Row.

Heim, Michael. 1994. *The Metaphysics of Virtual Reality.* New York: Oxford University Press.

Herrnstein, Richard J., and Charles Murray. 1994. *The Bell Curve: Intelligence and Class Structure in American Life.* New York: The Free Press.

Holtzman, Steven R. 1994. *Digital Mantras: The Language of Abstract and Virtual Worlds.* Cambridge, Mass.: MIT Press.

Idhe, Don. 1979. *Technics and Praxis.* Dordrecht, Holland: D. Reidel Publishing.

Illich, Ivan. 1970. *Deschooling Society.* New York: Harper & Row.

Jackson, Wes. 1987. *Altars of Unhewn Stone: Science and the Earth.* San Francisco: North Point Press.

Jacobson, Robert L. 1994. "Extending the Reach of 'Virtual' Classrooms." *Chronicle of Higher Education* (July 6): A19–23.

Johnson, Mark. 1987. *The Body in the Mind: The Bodily Basis of Meaning, Imagination, and Reason.* Chicago: University of Chicago Press.

Kay, Alan C. 1991. "Computers, Networks, and Education." *Scientific American* (September): 138–148.

Kelly, Kevin. 1994. *Out of Control: The Rise of Neo-Biological Civilization.* Reading, Mass.: Addison-Wesley.

Lakoff, George. 1987. *Women, Fire, and Dangerous Things: What Categories Reveal About the Mind.* Chicago: University of Chicago Press.

Lewis, Martin W. 1996. "Radical Environmental Philosophy and the Assault on Reason." Pp. 209–230 in *The Flight from Science and Reason,* ed. Paul R. Gross, Norman Levitt, and Martin W. Lewis. New York: New York Academy of Sciences.

Lewontin, R. C. 1992. *Biology As Ideology: The Doctrine of DNA.* New York: HarperPerennial.

Lumsden, Charles J., and E. O. Wilson. 1983. *Promethean Fire: Reflections on the Origins of Mind.* Cambridge, Mass.: Harvard University Press.

MacIntyre, Alasdair. 1984. *After Virtue: A Study in Moral Theory.* 2d ed. Notre Dame, Ind.: University of Notre Dame Press.

Mander, Jerry. 1977. *Four Arguments for the Elimination of Television.* New York: William Morrow/Quill.

———. 1991. *In the Absence of the Sacred: The Failure of Technology and the Survival of the Indian Nations.* San Francisco: Sierra Club Books.

Marglin, Stephen A. 1996. "Farmers, Seedsmen, and Scientists: Systems of Agriculture and Systems of Knowledge." Pp. 185–248 in *Decolonizing Knowledge: From Development to Dialogue,* ed. Frédérique Apffel-Marglin and Stephen A. Marglin. Oxford: Clarendon Press.

Minsky, Marvin. 1988. *Society of Mind.* New York: Simon and Schuster.

Moody, Roger, ed. 1988. *The Indigenious Voice: Visions and Realities,* vol. 2. London: Zed Books.

Moravec, Hans. 1988. *Mind Children: The Future of Robot and Human Intelligence.* Cambridge, Mass.: Harvard University Press.

Muir, Mike. 1994. "Putting Computer Projects at the Heart of the Curriculum." *Educational Leadership* (April): 30–33.

Mumford, Lewis. 1934. *Technics and Civilization.* New York: Harcourt, Brace, and World.

———. 1967. *The Myth of the Machine.* New York: Harcourt, Brace, and World.

———. 1970. *The Pentagon of Power.* New York: Harcourt, Brace, and World.

Negroponte, Nicholas. 1995. *Being Digital.* New York: Alfred A. Knopf.

Newby, Timothy J., Donald A. Stepich, James D. Lehman, and James D. Russell. 1996. *Instructional Technology for Teaching and Learning.* Englewood Cliffs, N.J.: Prentice-Hall.

Noble, David F. 1998. "Selling Academe to the Technology Industry." *Thought and Action* 14: 29–40.

Ong, Walter. 1982. *Orality and Literacy: The Technologizing of the Word.* London: Methuen.

Oppenheimer, Todd. 1997. "The Computer Delusion." *Atlantic Monthly* (July): 45.

*The Oregon Trail II.* 1993. Minneapolis, Minn.: MECC.

Papert, Seymour. 1980. *Mindstorms: Children, Computers, and Powerful Ideas.* New York: Basic Books.

———. 1996. *The Connected Family: Bridging the Digital Generation Gap.* New York: Longstreet.

Peters, Michael, and Colin Lankshear. 1996. "Critical Literacy and Digital Texts." *Educational Theory* 46 (Winter): 51–70.

Picard, Rosalind W. 1997. *Affective Computing.* Cambridge, Mass.: MIT Press.

President's Committee of Advisors on Science and Technology, Panel on Educational Technology. 1997. *Report to the President on the Use of Technology to Strengthen K–12 Education in the United States.* Washington, D.C.

Provenzo, Eugene F., Jr. 1991. *Video Kids: Making Sense of Nintendo.* Cambridge, Mass.: Harvard University Press.

Putnam, Robert D. 1993. *Making Democracy Work: Civic Traditions in Modern Italy.* Princeton, N.J.: Princeton University Press.

Rheingold, Howard. 1991. *Virtual Reality.* New York: Summit Books.

———. 1993. "A Slice of Life in My Virtual Community." Pp. 57–80 in *Global Networks: Computers and International Communication,* ed. Linda M. Harasim. Cambridge, Mass.: MIT Press.

Rifkin, Jeremy. 1995. *The End of Work: The Decline of the Global Labor Force and the Dawn of the Post-Market Era.* New York: G. P. Putnam's Sons.

Rohwedder, W. J., and Andy Alm. 1994. *Environmental Education Toolbox— Workshop Resource Manual: Using Computers in Environmental Education.* Ann Arbor, Mich.: School of Natural Resources and Environment.

Roszak, Theodore. 1994. *The Cult of Information: A Neo-Luddite Treatise on High-Tech, Artificial Intelligence, and the True Art of Thinking.* 2d ed. Berkeley: University of California Press.

Sachs, Wolfgang, ed. 1993. *Global Ecology: A New Arena of Political Conflict.* London: Zed.

Sagan, Carl. 1997. *The Demon-Haunted World: Science As a Candle in the Dark.* London: Headline.

Schorr, Joseph. 1994. "Learning Power: Software for Kids—Ten Rules for Choosing Educational Software for Your Kids." *MacUser* (December): 90–95.

Sclove, Richard. 1995. *Democracy and Technology.* New York: Guilford Press.

Scollon, Ron, and Suzie Wong Scollon. 1992. *Individualism and Binarism: A Critique of American Intercultural Communication Analysis.* Research Report #22. Hong Kong: City Polytechnic of Hong Kong.

Scott, James C. 1976. *The Moral Economy of the Peasant: Rebellion and Subsistence in Southeast Asia.* New Haven, Conn.: Yale University Press.

Shils, Edward. 1981. *Tradition.* Chicago: University of Chicago Press.

Shiva, Vandana, 1993. *Monocultures of the Mind: Biodiversity, Biotechnology, and the Third World.* Penang, Malaysia: Third World Network.

Shiva, Vandana, and Radha Holla-Bhar. 1996. "Piracy by Patent: The Case of the Neem Tree." Pp. 146–159 in *The Case Against the Global Economy and for a Turn Toward the Local,* eds. Jerry Mander and Edward Goldsmith. San Francisco: Sierra Club Books.

*SimAnt.* 1991. Orinda, Calif.: Maxis.

*SimCity 2000.* 1993. Orinda, Calif.: Maxis.

*SimEarth.* 1991. Orinda, Calif.: Maxis.

*SimLife.* 1995. Orinda, Calif.: Maxis.

Snyder, Gary. 1990. *The Practice of the Wild.* San Francisco: North Point Press.

Spretnak, Charlene. 1997. *The Resurgence of the Real: Body, Nature, and Place in a Hypermodern World.* Reading, Mass.: Addison-Wesley.

Sternberg, Robert J. 1990. *Metaphors of Mind: Conceptions of the Nature of Intelligence.* New York: Cambridge University Press.

Stock, Gregory. 1993. *Metaman: The Merging of Humans and Machines into a Global Superorganism.* Toronto: Doubleday Canada.

*Storybook Weaver.* 1993. Minneapolis, Minn.: MECC.

Thurow, Lester C. 1996. *The Future of Capitalism: How Today's Economic Forces Shape Tomorrow's World.* New York: Willam Morrow.

Turkle, Sherry. 1996a. *Life on the Screen: Identity in the Age of the Internet.* New York: Simon & Schuster.

———. 1996b. "Who Am We?" *Wired* 4 (January): 148–151.

Van Der Ryn, Sim, and Stuart Cowan. 1996. *Ecological Design.* Washington, D.C.: Island Press.

Visvanathan, Shiv. 1997. *A Carnival for Science: Essays on Science, Technology, and Development.* New York: Oxford University Press.

Wackernagel, Mathis, and William Rees. 1996. *Our Ecological Footprint: Reducing Human Impact on the Earth.* Gabriola Island, B.C., Canada: New Society Publishers.

Weizenbaum, Joseph. 1976. *Computer Power and Human Reason: From Judgment to Calculation.* San Francisco: W. H. Freeman.

Wilson, David. 1997. "The Appeal of Hypertext." *Chronicle of Higher Education* (September 28): A25.

Wilson, E. O. 1975. *Sociobiology: The New Synthesis.* Cambridge, Mass.: Harvard University Press.

———. 1978. *On Human Nature.* Cambridge, Mass.: Harvard University Press.

———. 1998. *Consilience: The Unity of Knowledge.* New York: Alfred A. Knopf.

Wilson, E. O., and Charles J. Lumsden. 1983. *Promethean Fire: Reflections on the Origins of Mind.* Cambridge, Mass.: Harvard University Press.

Winner, Langdon. 1986. *The Whale and the Reactor: A Search for Limits in an Age of High Technology.* Chicago: University of Chicago Press.

Woolfolk, Anita E. 1993. *Educational Psychology.* Boston: Allyn and Bacon.

Zeitz, Leigh E. 1996. "Is It Too Late to Offer Introductory Computing Workshops to Faculty and Staff?" *The Computing Teacher* (March) 33–35.

# Index

Abram, David, 35, 36
Academic community, 120–121; cultural
intelligence and, 125; ideology
promoted by, 55–56, 183; knowledge
and, 65, 66. *See also* Authority
Accountability, 32
Accounting, ecological, 67
Addictions, 66, 177
Advertising, 52–53, 99
Agriculture, 6, 50, 165; commodification
of, 95; genetic engineering, 52, 68;
impacts of technology, 67–68,
178–179; industrial model, 27;
traditional, 67, 68, 172; water
resources and, 51; work force
decline, 7; world trade and, 145
Alexander, Richard D., 89
Analogic thinking, 26, 27–28, 33, 123,
161
Andean cultures, 67, 144, 171–172
Anderson, Edgar, 95
Anthropocentrism, 12, 38, 128;
constructivism and, 148; in

cyberspace, 37; of educational
software, 137, 173; primary
socialization and, 157; as root
metaphor, 33
Anti-intellectualism, 103
Apache, Western, 38–39, 65
Apffel-Marglin, Frédérique, 95
Appiko movement, 53–54
Artificial Intelligence, 79
Assumptions, cultural. *See* Cultural
assumptions
Athabascan cultural groups, 42
Authority, 36, 97; of abstract systems
of representation, 55–56; of academic
knowledge, 174–175; of data, 71;
of individual perspective, 34; moral
(*see* Moral systems and relationships);
of science, 83–84, 85, 99–107
Automation, costs of, 16–17
Autonomy: heteronomy versus,
147–148; of individual, 32, 178;
intelligence as attribute of, 151,
152

205

implications of computer culture, 60–64; knowledge of place, 64, 68–69; of local knowledge (*see* Local knowledge); teacher awareness of, 164–165

Internet, 76–77, 117, 120, 151. *See also* Cyberspace

Jackson, Wes, 65, 68, 95
Jacobson, Robert J., 120
Johnson, Mark, 28
Judeo-Christian root metaphors, 26–27
Justice, social, 2, 189–190

Kay, Alan C., 80, 115–116, 147
Kelly, Kevin, 13, 78, 81, 82–83, 84, 87, 91, 92–93, 96, 97, 189
Kepler, Johannes, 27, 156
Knowledge, 103; academic computer experts and, 125; academic/formal versus traditional, 66, 74, 75, 174–175 (*see also* Authority); commodifying, 185; context and, 65, 66; craft, 7; and culture, 23, 150, 158–159; decontextualized, 158; degraded, data as, 47; and education, 56; epistemology, 83–84, 97, 174–175; experiential versus technological, 174; expert (*see* Expert knowledge); moral, 73–74; noncommercialized, 107; of place, 64–69 (*see also* Traditional cultures); privileged, 79; root metaphors of, 33–34; scientific method and, 83–84; society based on, 142; status and, 12, 55, 66, 73–74, 185, 190; symbolic, 24, 25. *See also* Contextual knowledge; Cultural forms of knowledge; Local knowledge
Kohlberg, Lawrence, 147, 149, 150

Lakoff, George, 28
Landscape, 38–39. *See also* Local knowledge
Language, 12, 23, 193; analogical process, 26; computer-mediated learning and, 123–124, 158; culture-thought-language relationships, 25, 29, 72–73, 123, 147, 156–158, 193; cyberspace, 18, 34; ecology of, 147; labeling of critics, 62, 103, 113, 150;

legitimation of elites, 157; and metacommunications, 9–10; metaphoric nature of, 25–29, 150 (*see also* Root metaphors); and modernity, 97; and moral codes, 37; Native American place names, 38–39, 65; and nonscientific knowledge, 84–85; oral interactions, 34–35, 62; teaching and, 161, 168; technology and, 4, 189
Lankshear, Colin, 117–118
L.E.A.R.N. Day, 140–141
Learning, 49, 127; constructivism and, 147–149, 150, 151, 152, 160, 164; context and, 65; lifelong, 126; software and, 132–133; student motivation and, 116. *See also* Education
Lee, Ann, 62
Lehman, James D., 126
Levitt, Norman, 99–100
Lewis, Martin W., 100–101
Lewontin, R. C., 90–91
Liberalism, 51–52, 55–56, 118; assumptions of, 101; and change as progress, 58; cultural bioconservatism and, 59; and educational theories, 148–150; individualism and, 178; teacher education and, 164
Liberation technology, computers as, 117
Local contexts, cultural bioconservatism and, 58–59
Local knowledge, 47; in agricultural practices, 95–96; commodification of community and, 74–75; vs. data, 54–60; devaluing of, 65–66; loss of, 17; mentoring and, 63; Nature and, 94–95; oral tradition and, 62; of place, 65–66; status of, 12; wisdom in, 59–60, 61
Loka Institute, 194
Low-context knowledge, 65
Low-status knowledge, 12, 55, 73–74, 185, 190. *See also* Cultural forms of knowledge
Luddites, 103, 113
Lumsden, Charles H., 88

Machine intelligence, 81
MacIntyre, Alasdair, 44–45, 65
Malpractice, educational, 111